THE SIX SUPERPOWERS WITHIN

ERIC STEPHENSON

ISBN (paperback): 979-8-218-82519-5

ISBN (ebook): 979-8-218-82522-5

Editing & Design:
Our Galaxy Publishing

For my Dad, the only hero I've ever had.

Edward Carter Stephenson
1936-2021

THE SIX SUPERPOWERS WITHIN

So What? Now What? Activate!

Superpower

[soo-per-pou-er]

noun

Your signature personal agency in the world that when activated intentionally will save you. It rapidly accelerates the health, growth, and restoration of all that's within and around you.

I'll never forget the chilling sound of my father's coffin clicking into the steel track of the hearse. As one of six pallbearers, I stood frozen in the cold, dark Upstate New York winter, my hands numb and my heart heavy. At that moment, a deep realization settled: "My life is never going to be the same." It was a piercing truth, one that reshaped my entire world.

The only hero I ever had in my life was now gone. As you can imagine, I fell numb for weeks.

In the following months, a deep reflection haunted me: Now what?

I made a commitment: "I'm going to finally write this book before it's my turn to ride in that hearse." And so, I did. The book you're holding now didn't come overnight. It took years—fifteen years, to be exact. But I'd learned that all change takes time. The important thing? I showed up, again and again, and eventually, the words poured out.

In the prose of poet Mary Oliver:

"What is it you plan to do with your one wild and precious life?"

As of the writing of this book, events are happening in the greater world that rival the most unbelievable, drama-filled Hollywood movies. Depending on how we interpret world events at any given point in history, we can see fact as stranger than fiction. Given this reality, I am compelled to ask one of my favorite coaching questions:

So what? Now what?

Well, there is nothing that is going to make life go away or stop it from happening. Goodness knows I could not stop my father from dying, or hide from the ripple effect that occurred in my world thereafter. This was an important acceptance. There is no finish line that we reach, no end to the drama, no end to love and joy, no end to abundance, no end to pain and suffering, no end to grief. It's all here—forever and ever. And we've got to keep it movin' through it all.

The first noble truth of Buddhism is that there is always suffering or dissatisfaction in life. Don't I know it! This does not mean life is one-dimensionally stressful or painful, but that feelings of unease, dissatisfaction, and discomfort are inherent in the human experience. This is because life is impermanent and subject to constant change. Such suffering is universal and cannot be avoided, even by fulfilling our desires. "If I have this… I will not suffer because…" is not a feasible hypothesis. This mindset could lead to more suffering. I ask again…

So what? Now what?

Well, we have options. In the most basic terms, we always have three choices in life:

1. Accept it.
2. Change it.
3. Leave it.

Remember, there is always a choice. We can choose to get stuck in the inevitable discomfort and uncertainty of life, starring in our own drama-filled script with no control over the plot, or we can claim agency over our lives and consciously choose how we carry ourselves. The latter does not offer us a life without suffering, but it gives us access to understanding suffering as a means of self-discovery.

Agency is about our ability to act and make choices. How we carry ourselves—our energy, our presence, our tone—is what I call comportment. It means that we have control over our decisions and actions and can influence outcomes in our lives or environments. Think of it as the power to act or self-determination. Comport is about how we behave or carry ourselves. It's more about our external presentation, our attitudes, and the way we conduct ourselves in a given situation. Think of it as our demeanor or how we present ourselves to the world.

The suffering I experienced with my father's passing could have crumbled me, and for a while, it did. I gave up much of my sense of agency, often stripping myself of making conscious choices and instead letting pain steer the wheel. Trust me when I say that how I was showing up in the world reflected that. I felt heavy, withdrawn, reactive. I let grief become the main character in my story.

But eventually, I had to ask myself: Have I ever changed because I was comfortable? Absolutely not. Have I only truly changed in the moments of severe discomfort and running into a brick wall? Absolutely.

I realized that even in my sorrow, I still had a choice. And that's the thing—we always do. We don't choose what happens to us, but we do get to choose how we meet it. That's where the unbelievable power of our agency lives. When we begin to consciously carry ourselves through the world again—with softness, with boundaries, with purpose—that's how we reclaim our comportment. That's where real superpower lies. This is the hero's journey, and the message underneath most of the world's enduring myths and legends.

The problem often is that our comportment is frequently at odds with our agency.

Agency is one of my favorite words and concepts. It's one we will refer to over and over again through these pages. Agency is the ability to recognize that we have a choice, even when it doesn't feel like it. It's the inner sense that says, "I'm not just reacting to life, I'm actively and consciously participating in it."

At its core, personal agency is our capacity to act with intention, rather than living on autopilot or defaulting to survival mode. It's what allows us to pause, assess, and choose our next move. It also allows us to do this consciously, not based on fear, conditioning, or the chaos around us, but based on our personal values, vision, and authentic voice.

Agency doesn't mean controlling everything. It means owning what we can control. When people lack agency, they often feel stuck, powerless, or like life is "happening to them." But when we activate your agency, we flip that script. Life starts happening through us. We become the author of our own story rather than a character waiting for someone else to write the next chapter.

In this book, agency serves as our launching pad for everything else—kindness, resilience, emotional regulation, and accountability. It all begins with believing that we have a say in how we move through and experience the world.

Many of us find it challenging to balance the two aspects of comportment and agency. It's hard not to be more concerned with how others perceive us rather than what truly benefits us internally. Finding the balance between external validation and intrinsic motivation is tricky. Many of us don't even know what we want or meaningfully take the time to figure it out. We may be in an endless cycle of constantly seeking to score points outside ourselves, whether through social media likes, workplace accolades, or validation from our partners and peers, rather than focusing on what makes us truly happy and healthy. (Read that sentence again.)

From a Western-culture perspective, society often raises us to think about the output rather than the input regarding our role in the world. We often reflect on what we "should" be doing instead of reflecting on the experience. The focus tends to be on societal expectations and predefined goals, diverting our attention from our inner development and the richness of life in the present moment. The pressure to conform to society's ideals about what we should be doing results in a lack of authenticity as we prioritize external standards over expressing our unique selves. It takes away our agency and still leaves us suffering. This tendency to prioritize output contributes to a collective mindset that values achievement at the expense of holistic well-being, autonomy, and genuine fulfillment. This all-too-familiar rat race keeps us from genuinely connecting with ourselves and others.

What I find most alarming is that a pervasive sense of loneliness and despair has reached epidemic proportions in our society. A study by Harvard University researchers found that 36 percent of Americans are experiencing "serious loneliness," and some groups, such as young adults and mothers with small children, are especially isolated. Contrary to the common perception of loneliness as the absence of others, it can persist even in the company of loved ones. When we cannot authentically connect with ourselves, we struggle to feel a sense of belonging in the world.

Central to this epidemic is the concept of being truly present in the moment, not in the past or future. Presence is the necessary ingredient of all your superpowers. The absence of authentic presence is a major source of interpersonal conflict. In a world dominated by constant distractions—phones, television, and other external stimuli—the gift of presence emerges as one of the most invaluable contributions we can offer to those who matter. In fact, I would argue it is our most valuable currency. Yet, we often struggle to genuinely engage, especially in a fast-paced, digital landscape. Are we neglecting our primary needs and prioritizing systems that hinder our capacity for self-determination and personal transformation? And still feeling lonely or isolated? Well...

So what? Now what?

If we are going to survive this life with any sense of peace or contentment, we have to stop outsourcing our worth to external systems that were never built with our well-being in mind. We have to reclaim our agency—not the kind that screams productivity or perfection, but the quiet kind that allows us to choose ourselves, again and again, even when the world is loud and demanding. And we have to get honest about how we carry ourselves. Not for applause, not for the feed, but for the sake of living in integrity with who we really are. And it's a tall order.

When my father died, much of my old skin fell away. The shedding revealed a truth I can't unknow: this life is fragile, fleeting, and fully ours to shape. His passing forced me to reckon with what I want to do with the time I have left. It became the catalyst not just for writing this book, but for living my life on purpose. That's what this is all about—how we choose to live, even in the face of what we cannot change. Herein lies our powerful agency.

Because despite all the effort to appear put together—to meet the expectations, play the roles, check the boxes—we're still often lonely as hell. We're disconnected from each other because we're disconnected from ourselves. We can't find belonging in the world if we haven't found a home inside your own life. And while I don't claim to have all the answers, I can say this: the more I've chosen presence over performance, truth over perfection, and aligned action over approval, the more at home I've felt—in my grief, in my joy, in my skin.

You're here. I'm here. Let's begin.

IT ALL BEGINS & ENDS WITH YOU

During my career, I've taught a workshop entitled "Creating a Respectful, Drama-Free Workplace." It is one of my most popular courses. At its core, it teaches adults how to act like adults at work with empathy, accountability, and resilience. When someone in the seat next to me on an airplane asks what I do for a living, I would inevitably talk about this intention and this workshop as the one I enjoyed most. Almost without fail, the person will say, "We could really use your help where I work." In some ways, this continual feedback has led me to write this book.

Drama is a ubiquitous, deceptively casual term in modern society, used to describe behavior in family relationships, friendships, work relationships, dating, politics (along with politicians themselves), and reality-based television. Drama comes in many forms: gossip, judgment, polarization, exclusion, favoritism, and gaslighting, to name a few. Although we theoretically understand what "drama" means, I realized there wasn't a working definition to accurately connote the concept. It's taken me years of tweaking to get it clear and concise. I've since formulated this:

> Drama is a negative, voluntary action or behavior draining precious resources of time, money, health, and harmonious relationships, creating unnecessary stress in your life.

A primary tenet of this book is that all drama (as defined) begins and ends with us. It is what we really have control over. We are manufacturing drama or not. We are allowing drama or not allowing drama. What follows is the story of the cause and effect of drama, how to cultivate the core values of our own drama-free life, and how to lead and sustain it.

Our lives will always contain elements of suffering, constant change, personal choice, and other humans—all of which can bring drama to the forefront. We can't avoid life, but we can figure out how to have a better relationship with it. In other words, "Don't fight the flowing river."

In many ways, this book is a manifesto of an approach to life that puts our mental, emotional, physical, and spiritual health at the center. And thus, our acceptance that nothing outside of ourselves can truly define a successful life. We do this by seeing beyond all the noise keeping us out of alignment and going back into our bodies to find our way through. As we change the structure of our inner life, the functionality of every aspect of our being will change.

A mentor once told me, "We teach what we most need to learn." If this is true, then as a teacher and messenger, I need to continually learn how to be more present, create safety for myself and others, be less judgmental, and continually improve with my own self-care. This spirit is present within these pages, and please know that I am your constant companion on the quest. While I have spent much of my adult life crafting drama-free environments, I in no way, shape, or form claim to be flawless in their execution. However, much of the work does itself when I can faithfully practice certain principles.

We need to understand that drama is not something that happens to us, but more so, what happens because of our reactions to external forces. We're not passive recipients of dramatic events; we're active participants because we have agency. Our responses to all the output shape the intensity and nature of the drama we experience. Our interpretation contributes to the narrative that unfolds in our lives. And let's be honest, sometimes it's fun to participate in drama, even if it's just watching it on reality television.

Whether through intense emotional experiences or tumultuous situations, the costs associated with indulging in drama encompass every aspect of our identity and existence. Being an active participant in drama emotionally exhausts us, causes conflict and strained relationships, impacts our physical health, and incites chronic stress and loss of productivity—I could keep going (and I will throughout the book)!

Society actively promotes a fast-paced and hectic lifestyle that gives us the perception that there is little time to prioritize our inner beings. It's constant clamoring for outward attention. "Pay attention to this! Or me! Or this product!" We think we have no control. So, stressful environments, technological distractions, and the emphasis on quick fixes and external solutions are where we often fix our gaze.

As you'll see in the model below, drama isn't just a feeling. Drama is a cascade with real costs.

The Causal Model of Drama

Together with a friend and colleague, Dr. Richard Osbaldiston, we came up with the Causal Model of Drama. Drama causes a chain reaction, often characterized by conflict, emotional turbulence, or chaos, and creates unhelpful stress in our lives. The difference between helpful (or "eustress") and unhelpful (or "distress") stress lies in how our body and mind respond to a challenge, and whether that stress response enhances or hinders our performance, health, and well-being. This unhelpful stress, in turn, can have a range of negative effects on our mental, emotional, and physical well-being. These negative outcomes might include anxiety, burnout, strained relationships, or even physical health problems.

As a result of these negative outcomes, there are costs—both tangible and intangible. These costs can be financial, spiritual, mental, and physical, but they can also be personal, such as damaged relationships, decreased quality of life, or missed opportunities for growth and happiness.

For some time after my father's death, I felt powerless, like I was watching my life unfold from a place I couldn't touch. Much of my body felt uncomfortably numb as grief stripped me to the bone. The world around me felt loud, demanding, and often frustrating. In the wake of loss, I struggled to hear my inner voice over the noise of the world mixed with the chaos in my head. The drama in my life didn't just increase; it defined me for a time. That is what unresolved emotion often does: it makes space for drama because the real work of feeling, checking in, and slowing down seems impossible. The fire is too hot…

In fact, this period of my life is where my anxiety completely took over. As someone who has suffered from anxiety since childhood, the visual representation of how acute my suffering was showed up visibly with my nail biting. While hard to acknowledge even after all this time, here is what my self-inflicted, damaged thumb looked like three months after my Father's passing.

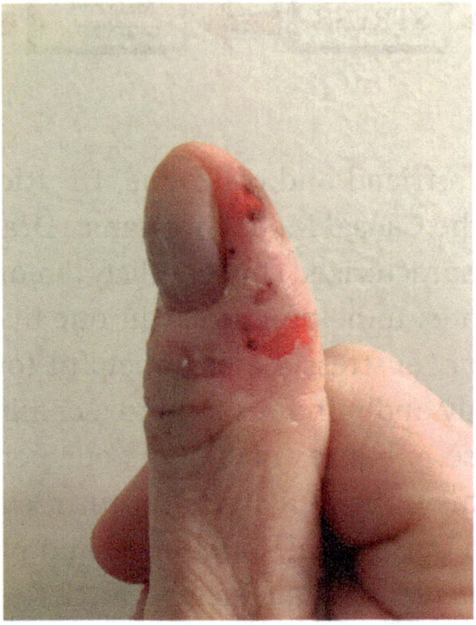

So often, we accept the cost of drama because we have no idea how to self-regulate our bodies. This was definitely the case for me. But how can we be expected to self-regulate when we don't even know how to check in? When we convince ourselves it's not worth our time? When we're taught to focus on what's wrong instead of right? Drama penetrates our lives when we allow it to be the focal point. We feed it with our egos and survival instincts even when we know it will only cause more stress. It becomes a comfort zone for us if we're accustomed to always living in it. Let's face it, there is a short-term high that often accompanies being difficult, demanding, and always right.

But we can choose not to indulge in it. As the drivers of our experiences, we have the agency not to engage, to actively steer clear of drama, and to promote a sense of sustainable and intentional living. To get there, we must ask ourselves:

What voice is leading me: the external circumstances or the internal wisdom and intuition I have always had within me?

It is possible to become bulletproof in our pursuit of an authentically fulfilling life when we let our wisdom and intuition lead us. Instead of relying on external interventions—or doing absolutely nothing about it—we could consciously practice methods of self-managing our bodies and maintaining a physiological state that keeps us in balance. We just need the tools to effectively listen and respond to the input rather than reacting to the output.

I recognize the complexity of this choice. I recognize the intricacies involved in dismantling our ingrained habits and conditioning amidst our fears about being ostracized, rejected, or judged for doing so. In our overstimulated survival brains, going against the grain means risking doing it "wrong." When we're honed in on the expectations of the external, it's hard to have faith in the internal. We lose trust in ourselves, in our ability to "just do it" without all the external noise. I also recognize we are here for the (often hard) work. You're ready!

Author Jerzy Gregorek proposed the notion of:

"Hard choices, easy life. Easy choices, hard life."

What he's conveying is that the difficulty of the decisions we make directly influences the overall ease or difficulty of our lives. Although challenging in the short term, choosing to face and make difficult decisions can lead to a more fulfilling life in the long run. When we opt for quick fixes, avoid challenges, or neglect our authenticity, we might receive temporary comfort, but we will only continue facing long-term challenges and hardships. Either way, we're suffering—even that is a choice.

At this point, we engage with drama to cope with difficult situations, even if it's not constructive. Without understanding what our body needs to manage its stressors, engaging with drama becomes a coping skill or even an addiction. Amidst our incessant need to garner external validation in a world that demands so much, dramatic behavior becomes a way to express ourselves and release all the intense emotions that come with navigating these human bodies. But it only leads to a deeper sense of insecurity within ourselves, perpetuating miscommunications and misunderstandings in our interpersonal relationships. We've allowed engaging with drama to be the easier choice to "handle" conflict rather than directly confronting why we react to external circumstances the way we do, and then choose differently.

As Elizabeth Gilbert said:

> "I've never seen any life transformation that didn't begin with the person in question finally getting tired of their own bullshit."

Isn't that where it all begins: taking responsibility for our role in the symphony of destruction? Once we take note of our self-deception, excuses, or negative patterns of behavior, we catalyze change from within. When we reach a point of recognizing and addressing our self-imposed obstacles and limitations, we can learn to engage with life without succumbing to the BS we used to allow to drive us. "The only way out of the drama is inside ourselves" becomes the mantra synonymous with the famous quote by Gandhi:

> "You must be the change you wish to see in the world."

To navigate life with greater ease and less stress, we've got to work on being responsive instead of reactive. We've got to take intentional steps instead of automatic responses that are not going to lead to measurable contentment. The key is to rebuild our self-trust and to reconnect with our safety nets instead of relying on that which is on the outside. We've got to find our Middle Path, one where we can make like Switzerland and find our neutral setting. Not go too high or too low, but meet ourselves right in the middle with honesty, compassion, and authenticity.

That's where the real work is, not in controlling every

circumstance, but in learning to control our responses to them. When we operate from the middle, we're no longer at the mercy of every external trigger. We're grounded. We can hear ourselves think. We can sense our feelings and tap into them. From that place, we make better choices that reflect who we truly are, not just who we're trying to prove ourselves to be. And to be frank, we can always choose the opposite of drama...

KINDNESS MEANS BUSINESS

If drama is everything I'm claiming it to be—a voluntary, negative behavior that drains our most precious resources—then what's its opposite? The kryptonite?

To me, it's kindness.

Not the watered-down, soft-spoken kind. Not the "be nice" variety that avoids conflict at all costs. I'm talking about the real kind, the kind that takes courage and guts. The kind that holds boundaries, speaks truth, honors nuance, and stays rooted when everything around us is trying to pull us off center.

Kindness is the UBERPOWER—the thread that connects the six core strengths we'll explore throughout this book. Without it, agency becomes control. Comportment becomes an "all the world's a stage" performance. Self-care becomes subtle narcissism. But with it? Everything aligns, softens, and strengthens.

Here's how I define it:

> Kindness is a positive, intentional behavior that protects and replenishes our most valuable resources—time, money, health, and harmonious relationships. It's the conscious choice to demonstrate empathy, accountability, and resilience.

It's the opposite of drama because it doesn't drain us. Conversely, it adds to our health, growth, and restoration as humans. It doesn't provoke unnecessary stress; it de-escalates and makes space for something new to emerge.

And make no mistake: kindness is strategic. It's not weak. It's not passive. It's one of the most powerful levers we can pull in both our personal lives and professional environments. It affects trust. It affects innovation, retention, performance, and well-being. It's the currency of real leadership and sustainable relationships. It affects the tangible key performance indicators (KPIs) of a business, especially the business of YOU! In a world obsessed with ROI, kindness might just be the most underrated investment we can make.

But more than anything, kindness is a conscious choice. It's one we make again and again, even when it's inconvenient. Especially when it's inconvenient. It's much easier to be kind when life is smooth and easy. It's another thing entirely to lead with kindness when we're under pressure, under-resourced, or emotionally raw. That's when kindness becomes an Uberpower. That's when it reveals who we are at our core.

Contrary to popular belief, kindness doesn't mean we don't feel anger, but it absolutely means we don't weaponize it. It doesn't mean we avoid conflict; we show up to it with clarity and compassion. It doesn't mean we agree with everything; we disagree without violent destruction. And, importantly, it doesn't mean we have to self-sacrifice. It means we honor ourselves while honoring another, and offer generosity from that grounded, centered place.

Kindness is the Middle Path that I will speak of in the next section. It's how we walk with presence, even when we want to run screaming out of the room. It's how we build real connection in the face of disconnection, how we restore dignity in a culture that tends to profit off division and shame. It's a portal into reclaiming our inner life from the noisy outer world.

And when practiced consistently—not performatively, but authentically—kindness becomes a force multiplier. It amplifies every inner capacity within us:

- It helps regulate our nervous system

- It builds deep trust and safety
- It anchors us in values and purpose
- It reinforces meaningful self-care
- It inspires aligned life design
- And it brings us home to contentment

Kindness isn't just the opposite of drama; it's the remedy. The return to the golden rule of sanity. The return to who we will always be beneath the noise. Kindness is both a practical strategy and an essential human faculty. It is our antidote to drama and the activator of our six core capacities.

So let it be known and anchor deeply within us…kindness isn't soft. It's Uberpower.

Let's walk the path together. We've got everything we need. Now it's time to remember it.

FINDING YOUR MIDDLE PATH

I once worked with an incredible wellness destination, Kamalaya, in Koh Samui, Thailand, for almost a month. During my stay, I befriended a server named Peet in the restaurant. Apart from perfecting *sah wah dee khrap!* (hello) and *laa gòn* (goodbye). I was unable to communicate verbally with Peet.

But non-verbally, we had been carrying on a conversation for weeks built on respect, admiration, appreciation, and laughter. We were kind to each other in every way. The day I left the property, he emphatically presented me with a small gift. A gift that has left a lasting memory in my head and heart. This one act of kindness left a meaningful, lasting impression on me.

What he gave me was a small religious relic and a handwritten, preciously misspelled note which read: "The Middle Path"

In Buddhism, the Middle Path is a concept that means avoiding going to extremes. It's about finding a balanced way to live, one that does not require excess or self-denial. It is a foundation of the Noble Eightfold Path that guides people to end suffering and achieve enlightenment. One may follow a path one can maintain over time, a path that does not consciously cause harm or suffering to oneself or others. Or a path that does not consciously cause drama or suffering to oneself and others.

Through the Middle Path, we manage the highs and lows. The better we become at mitigating the lows and moderating the highs, the healthier our outcomes will be. I think of the ancient Taoist parable known as the "Farmer Story," in this instance, which is often attributed to the teachings of Zhuangzi, a Taoist philosopher from the 4th century BCE. It is, to me, one of the best ways to encapsulate the core of the Middle Path. Though it has been retold in many ways, the basis of the story goes like this:

A farmer had a horse, and one day, the horse ran away.
The neighbors came to offer sympathy, saying,
"What bad luck!"

The farmer simply replied,

"Maybe so, maybe not."

A few days later, the horse returned, bringing several wild horses.
The neighbors exclaimed,

"What good fortune!"

Again, the farmer replied,

"Maybe so, maybe not."

Shortly after, the farmer's son tried to ride one of the wild horses, was thrown, and broke his leg.

The neighbors once again expressed their condolences.

The farmer responded,

"Maybe so, maybe not."

Later, the army came to the village to conscript young men for war, but because the son had a broken leg, he was spared.

The neighbors said,

"What luck!"

The farmer's response remained unchanged:

"Maybe so, maybe not."

This story captures the essence of neutrality, the wisdom of finding a middle ground, and the understanding that life's events are neither inherently good nor bad—they simply are. Every low tide gives way to a high. We often feel compelled to label our experiences as positive or negative and react accordingly. However, this reactive nature can lead us down a path filled with drama and stress.

The Chinese farmer is a prime example of not getting overly attached to the highs and lows. Good and bad outcomes change over time. Happiness comes, and happiness goes. When we find our state of neutrality, we preserve and align with the mental and physical energy we need to remain content.

Neutrality involves maintaining a balanced perspective, especially in emotionally charged situations. Instead of reacting with strong emotions, neutrality requires us to respond with calmness and equanimity. This is the core practice, the muscle that gets strengthened with every heavy lift.

Once we reduce the friction in our lives, we become free from the turmoil it manifests. In neutral, we are not tossed about on the sea of highs and lows. We are not controlled by our conflicts and suffering or the thoughts, emotions, and events that accompany them. We are in control. We know what it takes to remain steady on shaky ground. We can say with confidence, "This is what I want to do with my one wild and precious life," and need no validation for that decision. We just have to believe we're worthy of it. That we are absolutely deserving of the contentment we so desire, no matter what comes our way.

As we move through these chapters, keep the farmer's wisdom in mind. It will serve as a guiding principle as we delve into practices designed to bring us closer to that middle ground, that place of balance where we can respond to life's challenges with grace and resilience. This is where true healing and growth occur. Not in the extremes, but in the steady, centered place in between.

We don't need to be at the mercy of every emotional wave. We just need to find our center.

That's the Middle Path.

Think of it as more than just a concept from a distant philosophy. It's a life raft in the storm we're all navigating. It offers us a grounded response to the overstimulation, grief, loneliness, and identity crises that define the modern world. It is the antidote to the rat race, the drama loop, and the gnawing ache that tells us something's missing even when we've done everything "right."

The Middle Path doesn't ask us to renounce our ambition or pretend that pain doesn't exist. It invites us to build capacity for the in-between—to meet our suffering without being swallowed by it, to hold your joy without clinging to it, and to finally trust that presence is more powerful than performance. It's how we get out of the cycle of reacting to life and start relating to it instead.

This path is how I began to reclaim myself after the grief of my father's death nearly unraveled me. It's how I returned to my agency when the world felt like too much. It's how I stopped trying to prove myself and started living for myself. This path will meet us wherever we are—not with pressure to fix, but with permission to be. We don't have to be perfect. We just have to stay present.

We're not here to be perfect. We're here to be present on purpose. Let's meet our Superpowers and start living like we mean it.

My Thai friend, Peet will never know how much his small act of kindness touched my heart. That is the power of being kind; it echoes for long after.

Now that we've seen the terrain we're navigating—grief, presence, drama, kindness, I want to introduce the map that will guide us. But first, we need a compass…

YOUR TOOL OF MASS COMPASSION

Any person who's about to start a movement within themselves needs a compass of sorts, a tool to help them stay directed along their journey. For me, and now for you, it is the Sword of Superpowers. Rooted in Zen Buddhist philosophy, this sword, originally called the Sword of Compassion, is a mental and emotional tool to cut through illusions, ignorance, and attachments that lead to suffering. It's a symbolic weapon of wisdom, clarity, and compassion—qualities that, when combined, can transform our lives.

The Sword of Superpowers is not a weapon of destruction. It is a boundary-setting tool, a protector of integrity, and a compass that helps us navigate chaos without becoming it. It's the inner signal that says, "This isn't right," and the external action that follows: "I'm willing to protect what matters." Each of the Six Superpowers is contained within the blade, shaped by life, sharpened through practice.

Traditionally, it is depicted as a flaming sword. The powerful invitation here is to "take hold of the flame." The phrase "take hold of the flame" is particularly significant because it suggests that we have the power to wield this transformative tool with intention. Here, the metaphor of the sword becomes deeply personal. We all can engage with the challenges in our lives with clarity to discern the truth beneath layers of confusion or self-deception.

The sword helps us confront the truth head-on. It demands that we recognize our attachments—whether to beliefs, people, possessions, or habits—that lead to suffering. The concept of cutting through illusions is seeing beyond the BS. It's seeing beyond the surface-level appearance of things and recognizing our biases, judgments, and fears about ourselves and others. Cutting through these attachments with wisdom and compassion makes room for growth, peace, and more authentic living. We take action from a place of love, empathy, and understanding rather than aggression or fear.

This belief holds that great courage is not demonstrated by aggression or ambition but rather by truth. In this sense, the Sword of Superpowers becomes the perfect tool for the life we are fashioning. The sword allows us to shape our lives, our relationships, and our destinies with a deep commitment to the truth and a desire to alleviate ourselves from the drama. It allows us to take action in a way that is aligned with our highest values, moving through the obstacles that prevent us from living fully and authentically.

In the words of spiritual teacher Jack Kornfield:

> "The courageous heart is the one that is unafraid to open to the world, to care no matter what. With compassion, we come to trust our capacity to open to life without armoring. Compassion is not foolish. It doesn't just go along with what others want so they don't feel bad. There is a yes in compassion, and there is also a no, said with the same courage of heart. No to abuse, no to racism, no to violence, both personal and worldwide. The no is said not out of hate but out of an unwavering care. Buddhists

call this the fierce sword of compassion. It is the powerful no of leaving a destructive family, the agonizing no of allowing an addict to experience the consequences of his acts."

I was introduced to this concept when I was learning to become an instructor (and manage adults) by my mentor, Carey Smith. Like any skilled swordsman, I have practiced to great success and horrible blunders over the years. Believe me, the first couple of times I drew the sword, my hands were shaking. And yes, mistakes were plentiful in the early going.

Now, the sword is always with me. Right by my side, a constant, trusted companion. Yet, most of us don't even realize we possess one. We carry it, but often, we lack instruction on how to use it. Many wield it aggressively, without compassion. Others bury it altogether, avoiding confrontation. But the true power of the sword lies in balance—in wielding it with both wisdom and empathy. It comes from reflecting on the question:

Do I trust my capacity to open to life without armoring?

We draw this sword not to fight others, but to protect our integrity. To say "no" to abuse, shame, and untruths, not from hate, but from unwavering care. In moments of self-judgment, we draw it inward with tenderness, using it to sever our identification with the stories that keep us stuck.

YOUR SIX SUPERPOWERS WITHIN

Think of a tree. A tree doesn't doubt itself when the leaves fall in autumn or when the blossoms return in spring. It knows its role in each season. It sheds, stores, blooms, and bears fruit. Not to impress anyone, but because that's its design. Our bodies, too, hold that wisdom. But to access it, we need to slow down and listen.

We are all seekers, doing our best to grow and evolve in a world that rarely gives us time to pause. Even when it feels like we're stuck, our minds and bodies are always responding. Always adapting. Just like nature, we move through seasons—times of blooming, pruning, resting, and regeneration. But unlike the natural world, we often resist our own rhythms. We push when we should pause. We numb when we should feel. We sprint when what we need is stillness.

I initially created what I used to call the Drama-Free Philosophy as a way to see through the noise in my life and return to what mattered: alignment, clarity, and authenticity. But as my journey deepened—and especially through the lens of grief, self-trust, and healing—I realized this wasn't just about removing drama. It was about reclaiming power. Not performative, hustle-fueled power, but the kind that comes from a deep, quiet place within. The kind that helps us navigate suffering with grace and face life's uncertainty with grounded presence.

That's when this philosophy evolved into something more expansive. A guide for returning to our Middle Path. A framework rooted in balance, built to help us work with the full spectrum of our human experience—joy, grief, overwhelm, growth—without bypassing it or becoming consumed by it.

At the heart of this philosophy are six inner strengths, what I call our Six Superpowers within:

1. The Autonomic Nervous System
2. Safety & Trust
3. Vision & Values
4. Self-Care
5. Life Design
6. Contentment

These are natural, powerful internal resources already within you, waiting to be remembered, practiced, and embodied. When we tap into them, we stop living at the mercy of the outside world and start living from our center. These six elements help us reclaim self-trust, build emotional regulation, and reorient ourselves toward a state of contentment. They are how we walk the Middle Path, not with perfection, but with presence. Each chapter will explore one of these superpowers in depth, offering tools, practices, and reflections to help us embody each one in our daily life.

This book isn't about forcing growth. It's about aligning with our own rhythms so we can thrive in every one of our seasons.

1. YOUR AUTONOMIC NERVOUS SYSTEM (THE SEED)

Our nervous system is our body's command center. It regulates how we experience the world, whether we feel calm or chaotic, safe or threatened. Without a basic understanding of how this system works, we default to survival mode, often confusing high stress with high performance. This is the root of burnout, anxiety, and emotional disconnection.

But when we learn how to work with the nervous system instead of against it, we create the foundation for every other area of growth. This is where self-awareness begins, where we plant the seed of real change.

2. YOUR SAFETY & TRUST (THE ROOTS)

Nothing meaningful can grow without safety. Emotional safety. Nervous system safety. Relational safety. We all crave a sense of belonging and grounding. When we feel safe in our bodies and our environments, we trust ourselves more deeply. We take braver steps.

Just like roots stabilize and nourish a tree, a strong sense of internal safety and trust grounds us. It allows us to navigate life from a place of security rather than defensiveness. When we cultivate trust—especially in ourselves—we begin to rewire our relationship with risk, vulnerability, and connection.

3. YOUR VISION & VALUES (THE TRUNK)

Our vision and values are the backbone of who we are and what we stand for. Without a clear sense of purpose, it's easy to collapse under pressure or live by default rather than design.

Just as a tree's trunk supports its entire structure, our vision and values provide stability, strength, and direction. They help us stay upright when the winds of life blow hard. When we're deeply connected to our "why," we make decisions from alignment rather than fear or reaction. Our values become your compass. Our vision becomes our map.

4. YOUR SELF-CARE (THE BRANCHES)

Self-care is how our values take shape in the real world. It's not indulgence—it's integration. It's sleep, boundaries, joy, nourishment, rest, and repair. It's how we protect our peace and invest in our longevity.

Like the branches of a tree, self-care stretches outward into every part of our life. The more rooted and supported we are, the more gracefully we can reach toward our work, our relationships, our community. Without intentional self-care, even the strongest trunk begins to splinter. These practices aren't accessories to healing; they're an extension of it.

5. YOUR LIFE DESIGN (THE LEAVES)

Life design is about making conscious, aligned choices. It's how we turn our values into habits and your vision into structure. It's not about designing a perfect life—it's about building one that's sustainable, nourishing, and real.

The leaves of life design gather energy. They're the choices, commitments, and systems we put in place that keep us growing toward the person we want to be. When we design our life with intention, we stop drifting, and start creating.

6. YOUR CONTENTMENT (THE FRUIT)

Contentment is not a final destination, but a way of being that requires repetition and commitment. It's the quiet joy that comes from living in alignment, even when life isn't perfect. Unlike fleeting happiness, contentment is rooted. It comes from knowing that we are living truthfully, even in the mess.

Just as a tree bears fruit when all of its systems are working together in harmony, contentment arises when we're connected to our body, our needs, our purpose, and our path.

STAYING IN TUNE: THE EAR THAT KEEPS US LISTENING

Here's something else that's going to keep showing up throughout this book.

It's called The Listening **EAR**: *Empathy, Accountability, Resilience.*

Think of it like our inner compass. A way to check in with ourselves when the noise gets loud. A method to stay grounded, honest, and human as we grow through the messy, beautiful, unpredictable work of becoming ourselves. I developed it as a tool for listening to ourselves, our body, our instincts, and our truth. It is meant to help us notice what's showing up in our lives, how we're responding to it, and where we might be out of alignment with the life we actually want to be living. It's how we stay connected to the very things we're here to explore.

EAR is our way to pause and tune in before we react. It's how we ask better questions before we jump to conclusions. It's how we meet ourselves with honesty and care at the same time. It's meant to assess where we are, what we need, and what might be out of sync.

This isn't about fixing ourselves, it's about *listening* to ourselves clearly, consistently, and without judgment. Our Middle Path isn't out there. It's already inside us. It's within those Six Superpowers, and EAR just helps us hear it.

EMPATHY

Empathy is how we start soft with ourselves. It's is about understanding our own internal experience with compassion. When we're dysregulated, anxious, frustrated, or just over it, empathy asks, *"What's underneath this?"* not *"What's wrong with me?"*

Empathy is the gateway to self-awareness. We can't build new patterns if we're judging the old ones. So, as we begin examining our nervous system, our needs, our behaviors, start from here. Empathy makes change possible without shame driving the process.

ACCOUNTABILITY

Now we're getting real. Accountability is where we take ownership, not just of our actions, but of our patterns. It's not about blame. It's about ownership. This is where we ask, *"What am I choosing here?"* and *"Is that choice aligned with who I say I want to be?"*

We'll see this show up especially in how we respond to our nervous system, how we care for ourselves, and how we navigate discomfort. Accountability helps us stop spiraling and start recalibrating. It's about being honest enough with ourselves to shift.

RESILIENCE

And finally, resilience. Not the hustle culture narrative. Not the "just push through" kind. I'm talking about resilience that lets us fall apart and come back together, as many times as we need to. The kind that says, *"This is hard, but I'm still here."* The kind that lets us rest, recalibrate, and try again. The resilience that promotes human health, growth, and restoration.

Real resilience lets us fall apart and come back together, again and again. It's our ability to come back to our tools, values, truth, even when we've veered off course. Especially when we've veered off course.

I COULD HAVE WRITTEN THIS WHOLE BOOK ABOUT...

Presence. Or about kindness. My next one probably will. But presence and kindness aren't just ideas, they're experiences. They have to be felt, tested, forgotten, and remembered again.

So, instead, of offering the rules before we head to the next chapter, I'll offer two questions:

"How do I know when I'm truly present?"
"What does kindness look and feel like in and from me?"

The answers will change. They should. But asking? That's where our superpowers begin.

CHAPTER 1:

Activate Your Autonomic Nervous System – The Inner Control Panel

"Short of having people buffer their lives with tons of activities and perfect nutrition and perfect social interactions, people learning to control their autonomic nervous system is, I think, really the next step in our species' evolution. I really believe what we are seeing now in the world is a 'call to arms' if you will, or a request from Mother Nature to have everybody learn how to control their autonomic nervous system a little bit better or ideally, a lot better."

— Andrew Huberman

For the better part of two minutes, I was convinced someone was trying to break into my apartment and kill me. It only took two minutes for my nervous system to experience a state that would take me nearly 20 years to unwind.

I lay fast asleep as usual, with a fan and a white noise machine humming loudly to prevent any environmental noise. Suddenly, I was jolted out of bed by three loud, urgent pounds on my front door. I jumped out of bed and rushed to the front door to investigate. What happened next will be forever etched in the fabric of my brain.

Realizing no one was to be seen at the front door, I hurriedly went to the back door. As I lifted a single slot on the Venetian blind, I saw a dark shadowy figure slowly creeping a foot away from my door with a handgun that looked as big as they come. I immediately fell to the floor and crawled over to span the distance of my living room to grab the phone. For the next 120 seconds, I was convinced someone was trying to enter my house and kill me.

"There is someone at my back door who is trying to kill me!" I whispered urgently to the 911 operator. I could barely get the words out, my breath too shallow to speak. My nervous system was still believing I was about to die! Now, imagine my utter relief when the operator said, "Sir, that is a police officer at your back door." Slowly, my breath returned, and although the waves of fear receded, they never fully disappeared.

She explained that two individuals had cut the phone lines to my neighbor's house two doors down and broken in through the back door. She was sleeping on the couch and, once she woke up to the sound of her door being kicked in, ran screaming over to my front door and desperately pounded on it, pleading for help. The police came, and thankfully, no one was hurt.

However, the lingering effects of that night reflected on my subsequent behavior, with ongoing vigilance and a heightened sensitivity to what I assumed could be a potential danger. In other words, the trauma from those two minutes of believing I was about to meet my fate would leave a big scar on my autonomic nervous system (ANS). For years after, I would randomly wake up during the night in a panic and walk down to the front door to double-check it was locked and deadbolted. This would continue to other residences where I would double-check the alarm, garage door, and any barrier I perceived would keep me safe. This is a perfect example of how my experience created a lasting imprint on me through my sympathetic (fight/flight/freeze) nervous system.

Now, I'm not here to give an in-depth scientific breakdown of how the nervous system works. I do not claim to be an expert on these processes, nor am I interested in convincing anyone that they need to be an expert to change their lives. We don't have to know the intricacies of electricity to use it; we only need to know how to turn on the light switch that illuminates the room. My focus is on helping people recognize that understanding this inner system governing our responses to stress, trauma, conflict, and drama is key to managing these situations effectively. Once we understand how the ANS functions, we can choose to work with it and move forward toward a harmonious life. I encourage it to become our new BFF.

Of all the chapters, I would label this one as "Top Priority." Learning about what the autonomic nervous system is, what it does, and how to regulate it has had a grand impact on all aspects of my life. It is working with this very system that drove me to create a drama-free life.

SURVIVAL MODE: A HARDWIRED AND ACTIVATED ANS

Here's the thing: Humans are hardwired to survive. We are born with primal instincts that act as the driving force of our unconscious self-preservation. We've been activating these innate, automatic behaviors since the beginning of time, rapidly perceiving threats and responding quickly to potential dangers around us. Think survival of the fittest. As a species, we gradually adapt to our environments by acquiring and inheriting behaviors that enhance our ability to stay alive.

These hardwired behaviors become deeply ingrained and genetically programmed into our biology. They're protective actions that occur without our conscious thought, designed to ensure our basic needs and safety measures are met to sustain our well-being. We don't need to question why we do them or where they came from (even though we should); our bodies are responding and reacting for us.

Much like how the banging on the door in the middle of the night jolted me out of bed in fear, instantly on high alert as my brain associated those bangs with danger. As I ran across the living room to investigate the sound, I never had a conscious thought of, "Should I be fearful or calm right now?" or "I wonder how I should handle this situation…" All I knew was my body felt threatened, my operating system switched to survival mode, and I responded. I responded out of pure, primitive instinct.

We're all running off a subconscious operating system that oversees these instincts and reactions. We know it as the autonomic nervous system (ANS). The ANS is the part of the nervous system that automatically regulates essential bodily functions like heart rate, digestion, and breathing without conscious effort. It is constantly working behind the scenes, shaping how we react to stress, connect with others, and navigate life. It's broken down into two main branches:

- **Sympathetic Nervous System:** Activates the body's "fight, flight, or freeze" response, increasing heart rate, energy, and alertness in response to stress or danger.

- **Parasympathetic Nervous System:** Controls the "rest and digest" response, promoting relaxation, recovery, and energy conservation.

It's helpful to have a roadmap laid out by an expert, and for that, I have always favored the work of Dr. Stephen Porges, a neuroscientist, psychophysiological researcher, and professor. He is the founder of what is known as the Polyvagal Theory, a concept used to help people understand the ANS and how it influences our behaviors, emotions, and social interactions based on safety cues (something we'll talk more about in the next chapter). He points to the idea that the ANS operates in a three-tiered hierarchy, moving between states of safety, action, and shutdown depending on what we perceive in our environment. Here's an overview of his work:

VENTRAL VAGAL SYSTEM (SAFETY & CONNECTION: THE SOCIAL STATE)

This is the newest and most evolved part of our parasympathetic nervous system, responsible for feelings of safety, connection, and calm. It is regulated by the vagus nerve—our body's built-in social engagement tool.

- When this system is active, we feel secure and connected, making communicating, reading social cues, and building trust easier.
- It helps downregulate stress, allowing us to clearly think, be creative, and problem-solve.
- This is the state where we thrive—where relationships, learning, and emotional well-being flourish.

SYMPATHETIC NERVOUS SYSTEM (FIGHT OR FLIGHT: THE ACTION STATE)

This system kicks in when we sense a threat, getting us ready to take action. It increases heart rate, blood pressure, and adrenaline levels, preparing the body to fight or flee.

- It's not necessarily a bad thing because it's what helps us react quickly in dangerous situations.
- However, when this system stays activated for too long without relief, it can lead to chronic stress, anxiety, and burnout.
- Our goal isn't to eliminate this response but to recognize when it's happening and bring ourselves back to balance.

DORSAL VAGAL SYSTEM (SHUTDOWN & FREEZE: THE SURVIVAL STATE)

This is the oldest and most primitive part of our nervous system, designed for extreme survival situations. When the body perceives a threat it can't escape, this system shuts everything down to conserve energy and protect us.

- When activated, we might feel numb, disconnected, or frozen, like we've checked out emotionally or physically.
- This can be useful in moments of extreme danger, but chronic activation can lead to depression, burnout, and trauma responses.
- If we've ever felt like we just "can't deal" and want to shut everything out, this system is at play.

So, basically, the Polyvagal Theory helps us understand how the ANS governs our reactions to the world around us, shifting between states of safety, action, and shutdown. The key here is that our bodies are constantly processing safety cues. If we feel safe, we're in a connected, calm state, where we can thrive. But when danger is perceived, our body shifts into fight, flight, or freeze mode to protect us.

By understanding how our nervous system moves through these different states, we can stop thinking of stress as an "on or off" switch. Instead, we learn to navigate between these states with more awareness, helping ourselves and those around us feel safe, supported, and at our best.

The banging sound I heard triggered the activation of my autonomic nervous system without me even knowing it. The sympathetic branch kicked in as I responded to the perceived threat. My physiology instantly changed. My heart pounded, my breath got shallower, and the alert signals in my body were heightened like they never were before, all to prepare my body to either confront (fight) the threat, escape from it (fly), or do nothing (freeze). My ANS orchestrated rapid and instinctive responses to keep me alive in that situation. Like when I fell to the floor and crawled to grab the phone to call for help. My nervous system did what it needed to do to keep me alive, all while on autopilot. (Thanks, natural selection.)

We could say the parasympathetic branch took over from that point. My body did enter a form of rest and digestion as I gradually began to relax. My heart rate slowed, my breathing regulated, and my body no longer felt like I could be killed at any moment. The fear receded enough for me to feel some semblance of normalcy in my body, but the long-term effects of that event completely altered the operating system of my ANS.

Within the operating system of our ANS, there is a coding process. We've got:

- **Positive codes:** Things that make us feel safe (keeping our parasympathetic nervous system in balance).
- **Negative codes:** Things that pose a danger or threat to us (things that trigger our sympathetic nervous system).

These codes inform us how to respond to situations, people, and things in our environment based on our body's association with that code. When negative codes are activated, we're in a stressed or high-alert state of arousal. When positive codes are activated, we are in a relaxed or calm state of arousal.

Though the system itself is subconsciously run, we do consciously build on this coding process with each experience we have. Our amygdala is at the center of this coding and is involved in the processing and interpretation of emotions, including anxiety and stress. It's like a tiny guard in our brains that helps us know when something might hurt us. Negative experiences, thoughts, and emotions become negative codes that we store in our operating system, telling us we must avoid or use caution against anything that resembles that negative code. If we don't, our sympathetic nervous system, or the dorsal vagal system, will ring its alarm. The same goes for positive ones. Where things feel safe or inviting to us, we are more inclined to lean in (even if it hurts us later), which helps regulate the parasympathetic nervous system, or the ventral vagal system.

The thing is, we can't outthink anxiety with logic because the amygdala doesn't speak that language. It doesn't care how many statistics we know or how hard we try to "stay positive." It only responds to the emotional code attached to our thoughts. For some, it's flying. For others, it's public speaking. If a thought has been tagged with fear or lack of control, our nervous system will react as if we're in danger every time.

The event I experienced reorganized my coding process, creating persistent thoughts and fears related to that potential threat. My coding was shifted. My autonomic nervous system had now developed a new, automatic code associated with safety at bedtime: incessantly triple-checking locks and disrupting my sleep to be sure I wasn't in danger.

I didn't know this then. If I did, it wouldn't have taken me 20 years to regulate my ANS after the experience. But that's the thing about this little almond-shaped part of our brains. All the amygdala knows to do is process, interpret, and react. That's its job. Without our conscious intervention, it's just continuing to react and respond through whatever branch of the system it thinks needs to be in control to keep us safe and alive.

Short-term survival reactions have long-term effects, just like they did in the aftermath of the incident in my home. My amygdala formed and stored emotional memories that influenced all my behaviors and reactions when it was time to go to sleep. Anything associated with that situation would occasionally trigger my fear and trauma. The more I reacted through the negative code of those memories, the more dysregulated my ANS became (until I intervened).

When the ANS is dysregulated, it can lead to physical and emotional imbalances. This can include things like increased heart rate, digestive issues, anxiety, fatigue, and difficulty managing stress, all of which disrupt our daily functioning and health (we'll discuss this more shortly).

It took a lot of inner work to rewire the coded memories my amygdala formed about anything associated with the experience in my home that evening. I had to challenge a massive amount of encoded behaviors and thoughts, confronting and processing a lot of emotions I had allowed to become deep-rooted in my psyche based on what had happened.

The keyword here is *allowed*. Although the ANS operates autonomously as a protective structure, its functioning can be modulated by our conscious influence. I'll repeat that again: it can be modulated. This is a crucial cornerstone of designing a drama-free life.

At this point, it may be helpful to ask yourself:

> What traumatic experiences, thoughts, and emotions have become negative codes that I am storing in my operating system?

Chances are, we each have quite a few. Perhaps some that we didn't even realize we were storing.

It's crucial to start assessing these codes and becoming an active participant in noticing them when they arise because only then can we begin to change them. Our ability to code these experiences means we also have the power to uncode them, but we can't do that until we recognize them. By consciously identifying which codes are influencing our reactions—whether positive or negative—we can intervene and begin the process of reprogramming. The key lies in recognizing these triggers as they emerge, allowing us to take control, heal, and ultimately reshape our response patterns for a more balanced, empowered life. Remember, we do have agency over this system.

YOUR CONSCIOUS ROLE IN THE BUSINESS OF YOU

Basically, we are the boss of our ANS system. The CEO. The top dog. The one who oversees the way it functions. When things go wrong in the business of us, all the ANS knows to do is process, interpret, and react based on whatever codes it associates with that wrongdoing. Whatever's in the employee handbook of survival is what it's going to do. Unless we intervene and instruct it otherwise, it's just going to keep repeating the same cycles (and we all know a thing or two about repetitive cycles).

Right now, we may be collectively acting like bosses who don't know any of our employees' names, are neglecting their working conditions, but check in just to make sure the numbers are good enough to keep the business flowing—if we get around to it. We probably haven't trained the team or chatted with them regularly to get to know the way they innately work.

All we know is that the ANS is hardwired to keep the business (us) alive. That's great. We need that. Alive is a start. But we can stay alive with chronic stress from high cortisol levels due to all of our unexamined triggers. We can stay alive with insomnia due to a lack of sleep from all the adrenaline that keeps us on high alert. We can stay alive and be sick, unhappy, and unfulfilled.

Staying alive, quite frankly, is the bare minimum. If you're reading this book, you're not just looking to stay alive; you're looking to create a life where you feel in control of your agency, your body, and your experiences without letting all the external noise and static impact your internal being. One major way to accomplish this is by being a better boss of this system. Ideally, much better.

The number of external situations that impact our ANS is not due to the system itself. It's not even because of the external situation. BS just happens. There is an endless array of circumstances we are all exposed to that are completely out of our control. Some are more personal, and others we universally experience. We cannot control when someone might bang on the door in the middle of the night and send our bodies instinctively into a panic. We can't control when someone might threaten our safety. We can't even control the ANS that runs throughout our bodies to protect us. Even that, to some degree, has its autonomy (hence the name).

When it comes to the inner workings of our ANS, we know it runs on autopilot. We can't control the fact that it's running. What we can control is the way we interact with how it runs, which, in turn, changes the functionality of its involuntary system. The more we nurture the team that helps us function, the better the entire corporation (we) will be.

Rather than trying to control the uncontrollable, our focus has to be on managing our conscious thoughts, emotions, and behaviors in response to them. The internal disconnect we feel when our ANS is dysregulated is not due to external circumstances or a faulty internal operating system. It's because we are not consciously focusing on a better way to respond and work with them. We're letting either the external circumstance or the internal, dysregulated system lead us. Not only is our conscious being not in charge when we do this, but we're also not effectively supporting the circumstance or the system. It can't be one or the other. It's got to be us, the conscious being, as the boss, working with both internal and external forces.

How we interact with those things is up to us. We can choose to let the uncontrollable control us and suffer the long-term effects of not being in charge. Or, we can decide to be an active, conscious, and intentional participant in running the ecosystem of our lives. We've heard variations of this. *Change your thoughts, change your life* is a similar concept to the one I'm articulating. By shifting our thoughts, beliefs, and attitudes towards a situation, we can alter our perception of it and consequently change the way we experience and respond to it. What I'm proposing is that we consciously prioritize our ANS to make those changes and create that shift.

Here, it is valuable to pause and reflect for yourself:

> Am I consciously working toward managing my conscious thoughts, emotions, and behaviors in response to things beyond my control?

At all levels of our society today, there is an amygdala war continually going on. Many of us are divided into opposing camps where fear and emotional reactivity drive us rather than rational discourse and authenticity. Many people are engaged in a constant struggle related to fear and stress. We're each facing some form of ongoing battles or conflicts driven by emotional responses, power struggles, and interpersonal dynamics. It impacts every aspect of our existence: emotionally, physically, mentally, and spiritually. We are not effectively in charge, and it shows. But I truly believe that a small, dedicated group of us holding this book can make a major impact.

Our ability to be less reactive to external stimuli, especially when we don't agree with them, is the work of brave adults. Herein lies so much of our personal agency. By getting to know the ANS, learning how to engage with it, and understanding what it means to keep it in balance, we are given the tools to make those life changes we're seeking sustainably. Whatever that looks like for us. We're allowing ourselves to get back to authenticity. It's an inside job. To work from the inside out for a change. If not, we risk navigating a life we should feel in charge of but don't.

And I've got to remind you, the risks are large.

THE COSTS OF AN ANS GONE ROGUE

Let's go back to that causal model I mentioned:

Drama leads to stress, which leads to negative outcomes, which leads to costs.

When the ANS is dysregulated, it means the branches within the system aren't working together as they should. They're not functioning properly to support our well-being. In a constant state of heightened arousal and hypervigilance from an overactive sympathetic system, it becomes more difficult to regulate our emotions. This results in chronic stress, anxiety disorders, and high blood pressure. Stress releases cortisol and adrenaline, activating the SNS and increasing heart rate and blood pressure. The more we stress, the harder this system works, straining our heart and blood vessels while weakening our resilience to disease and increasing our likelihood of depression, anxiety, and social isolation. (Because who can function under those conditions?)

Let it be known that cortisol is a hormone crucial to our body's stress responses. When we encounter stressful situations—emotional, mental, or physical—our body releases cortisol as a natural response mechanism. It's meant to mobilize energy reserves, increase heart rate, sharpen our focus, and prepare us to deal with the stressor (or threat) at hand. It also regulates blood sugar, supports immunity, and controls our metabolism. While essential, prolonged high cortisol levels throw our system into chaos.

Here's where things get even trickier: when our sympathetic nervous system is fully engaged, our brain's executive function goes offline—literally. The prefrontal cortex, responsible for rational thinking, problem-solving, and impulse control, shuts down in favor of survival mode. We lose our internal Wi-Fi connection. Decision-making, self-regulation, and long-term planning take a backseat as our brain prioritizes immediate threats, real or perceived. This is why, in a state of stress, we react rather than respond, often making choices we later regret.

It isn't difficult to recognize how prevalent this dysregulated state is within all aspects of our society. We first must recognize how prevalent it may be within our own body and then work to continually recognize it outside of ourselves.

Prolonged stress overworks the SNS, keeping it in a heightened state of alertness and disrupting balance with the parasympathetic nervous system (PNS). This constant activation weakens the immune system, making the body more susceptible to infections and inflammation. It also drives us toward unhealthy coping mechanisms. We turn to food, leading to obesity and diabetes. We smoke to relieve stress, damaging our respiratory system. We numb ourselves with alcohol to escape the discomfort. And we project our internal turmoil onto the world around us because we don't know how to process it.

Having an underactive parasympathetic nervous system has its own consequences like digestive issues, poor sleep (don't I know it), and difficulty relaxing. We can't even expect a healthy bowel movement when this system is out of sync. Insomnia and chronic restlessness take hold. The PNS also plays a key role in sexual function, supporting blood flow and relaxation. Reduced activity here can lead to a decrease in libido, arousal, and overall enjoyment of intimacy.

A dysregulated ANS doesn't just affect our body. It impacts our relationships, experiences, and opportunities. Emotional instability makes us more irritable, guarded, and hypersensitive. We become disconnected from ourselves. With anxiety and depression looming, building and maintaining relationships becomes an uphill battle. Cognitive function declines, and our focus, concentration, memory, and decision-making skills suffer. The ability to make sound judgments? That goes out the window.

Here is how this has historically played out in my life behind the wheel of a car: It's 7:30 in the morning, and I am driving on a four-lane highway to an engagement. I have James Taylor on the radio, a cup of Starbucks dark roast in my hand, and I am marveling at the sunrise in the distance. Life is grand! Cruise control is set at 72, and I am, in some ways, relaxed. Suddenly, out of nowhere, a motorcycle speeds past me at 95 miles an hour and cuts right in front of me to enter my lane and narrowly make it to the exit ramp. All at once, my body is flooded with cortisol and adrenaline. My amygdala asks one question to my ANS: fight, flight, or freeze?

If you are a good New Yorker like me, you find yourself stepping on the gas in your four-thousand-pound automobile to chase after the individual who just put your life at risk. (When is that ever a good idea?)

Honestly, I have had to work very hard in therapy and self-development to identify the following: Who and what pushes my buttons?

Now, my buttons are going to be different than yours. One of my big buttons has always been when I perceive another human doing something reckless on the road, putting my life in danger. So, at some point, I realized the danger of my amygdala response (road rage—let's call it for what it is) and decided to interrupt the drama that driving causes me. The first step was being aware of my conditioned response and then consciously choosing something different.

Balancing the nervous system in times like this is a serious matter, maybe the one between life and death out on the highways and byways of the world. Without a balance in our ANS, we can't respond appropriately to stressors when needed or return to a state of rest afterward. We, instead, become the host of a slew of physical, emotional, psychological, and social issues because our negative codes remain unexamined and in control. Our survival (flight, flight, freeze) brain becomes the forerunner for our decision-making.

Not achieving at least some level of mastery over our own ANS, and in turn, our physiology, could have immense implications on our health, well-being, and overall medical practices. This is not something that can be done overnight, nor is there a timeline or step-by-step instructional manual for doing it effectively. There is no one way. But that's the beauty of it. Instead of expending all of our energy trying to overwork our way into a one-size-fits-all approach to what our external world says is best for us, we get to design our own life approach.

But first, we must admit we are where the problem starts.

ON OWNING YOUR PART IN THE DRAMA

One of the keys to managing drama is internally training our bodies to know that no one ever dies from experiencing an emotion. The embodiment of anxiety would have us believe the exact opposite, that the emotion itself is dangerous and should be avoided at all costs. This is not true. Circumstances occur beyond our control. Fine. But we're in control of how we react to those circumstances. Since that is a fact, the way those circumstances impact us is our responsibility. Things will happen, but how they influence us (and our internal systems) requires our ownership.

I realize that this might seem like a broad statement. Some might be saying, "But Eric, trauma hurts. My trauma was not my fault. I can't help but let it impact me at times." I recognize this, too. Let me say that taking ownership does not mean accepting any sort of blame. Nor is it the expectation that you'll regulate your ANS and never deal with trauma triggers again.

Regulating our ANS and controlling the impact of situations beyond our control does not mean we don't feel our pain. We feel a whole lot of it when we first decide to work with this system because we have to face it. This time, we're feeling the pain to move through it, not against it. Acknowledging and nurturing our pain is an essential part of the regulation process.

Most of our pain is deep-rooted. Lots of our trauma comes to us through our childhood experiences, sometimes even as early as birth. Some of it might even be unconscious to us at this point in our lives, embedded deep into our coded memories that have been pushed to the back of our brains. But they still live through us if left unexamined. And whether it gets examined or not is the responsibility of…

You guessed it. You.

We've got to become aware and acknowledge where we are imposing pain on ourselves and others. Understanding and working with this system necessitates immense levels of self-reflection. It requires us to shift the narrative away from "This is affecting me" and toward "I am allowing this to affect me."

THE DRAMA TRIANGLE

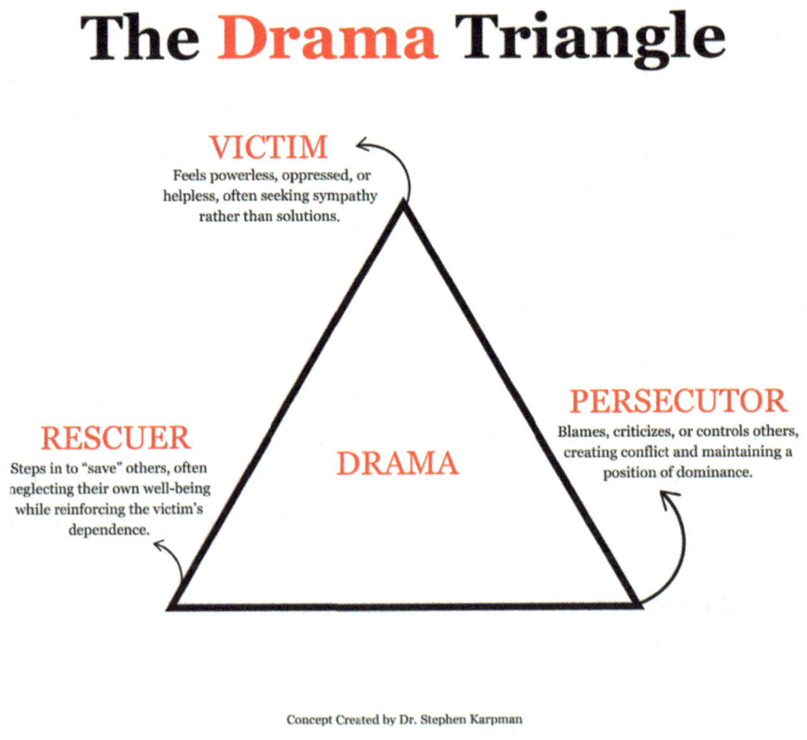

When it comes to drama, we usually fall into one of three roles: victim, persecutor, or rescuer. This is the Drama Triangle, a model created by Dr. Stephen Karpman to map out how people unconsciously participate in conflict. It shows us not just how we behave with others, but how we view ourselves when stress and emotional chaos take the wheel.

Each role tells a story. The victim sees themselves as powerless and stuck. They often seek safety through disempowerment ("If I can't help myself, no one can expect me to"). The persecutor controls, criticizes, or blames to regain a sense of dominance. They're the ones who will most likely seek safety through control ("If I dominate, I won't be hurt"). The rescuer steps in to "save" others, often abandoning themselves in the process. They're seeking safety through self-neglect ("If I stay needed, I'll stay loved").

Most of us bounce between these roles without realizing it. And when we do, our autonomic nervous system is usually running the show, perceiving threat where there may be none, and pushing us to react rather than respond.

The triangle helps us see where we contribute to conflict, manipulation, and unhealthy interactions. We start to recognize the patterns we lean toward and increase our self-awareness about how to move with them so they do not become who we are. Whether it's to assert boundaries, communicate more clearly, or take responsibility for our own emotions and actions, it is our job to navigate what role we're playing.

Until we're willing to lay all the cards on the table and take ownership for every crappy hand we think we've been dealt, well, then the rest of this book is all a moot point. Without acknowledging our role in the drama and destruction in our lives, we'll never be able to self-regulate the system that's making our decisions in these situations. We've got to take ownership of the triggers that keep us in an unbalanced state of being.

Once again, this does not mean we are to blame for them. Blame implies a fault, often accompanied by feelings of resentment, judgment, or condemnation that we're already doing too much of. We are not at fault for the things that happened to us that created negative codes in our amygdala. We are not to blame for being born into a society that doesn't prioritize this type of body awareness or conversation.

Unless we seek to learn on our own or are exposed to people close to us who specialize in these types of conversations, we'd have no idea. We live in a puritanical society with a cultural and social environment characterized by strict moral codes and outdated values that strip us of our ability to prioritize our body in all its forms. With all this enforced conformity and suppression of individual freedoms in today's world, we've been hell-bent on survival against all the external nonsense.

We all have these narrow standards we're expected to fit into. It's stifling creativity, authenticity, and personal autonomy. We fear judgment, so we constantly feel shame and guilt, contributing to a mental health crisis and a socially divided world. We're hindering our individual and collective progress and destroying any shot at empathy (both for ourselves and others).

So, no, I don't think blaming the individual does us any good. There's a societal dissonance, a misalignment between 1) the values drilled into our heads and 2) the resources we're given to uphold them. The powers at bay claim to prioritize moral righteousness while downplaying all the proof that the average human is overworked, overstressed, and forced into a system that does not prioritize their well-being.

I recognize that it's rough out here. But there is an admission to be had for being active participants in the drama. There is a need to admit to ourselves that we play a role in how we let life affect us and perpetuate the misaligned systems (internally and externally).

Take a minute here. Sit with it. If we really want to move through the rest of this work honestly, we have to ask ourselves:

- Which seat on the Drama Triangle do I usually plant myself in? Victim, persecutor, rescuer?

- Where do I tend to land when the mess hits the fan? And more importantly, why?

There's no shame in the answer. There's only information. Information we need if we're ever going to learn how to stop reacting out of old wounds and start responding from a place of power.

THE RHYTHM OF CHANGE

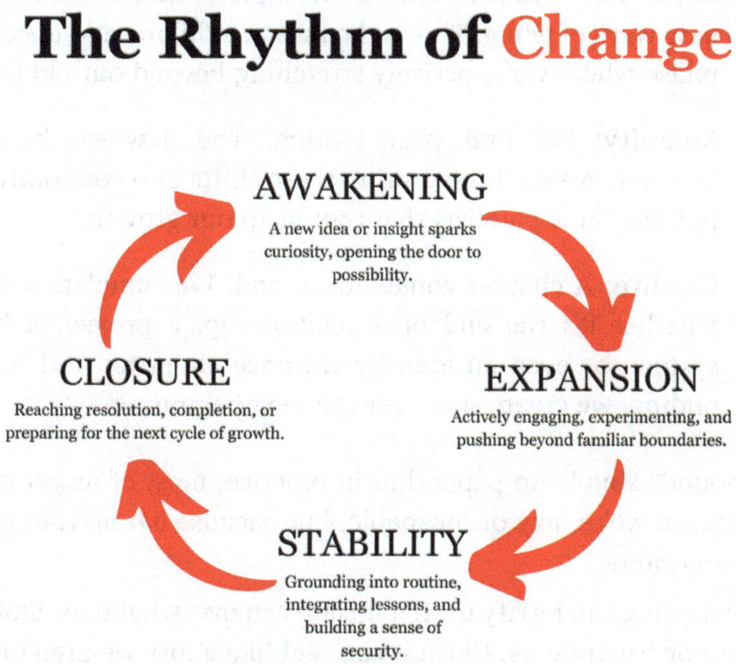

Concept Created by Richard Strozzi-Heckler

Part of owning our role in the drama is knowing where we stand in the natural process of change itself. It's one thing to realize we need to evolve, and another thing entirely to move through the discomfort it requires. Change, like anything alive, moves through a rhythm. Richard Strozzi-Heckler, a leader in the somatic field, mapped this rhythm in what he calls *The Anatomy of Change.* It flows through four stages: awakening, expansion, stability, and closure.

And every time we face growth, internally or externally, we move through some version of these stages. It looks something like this:

- **Awakening:** A new possibility appears. Something sparks inside us, like a realization, a longing, or a shift in awareness. We recognize that something has to change, even if we're not sure how yet.
- **Expansion:** We lean into it. We explore, take risks, and test new ways of being. This is the messy, exhilarating, uncertain phase where we're actively stretching beyond our old limits.
- **Stability:** We find your footing. The newness becomes familiar. We start integrating these shifts into your daily life, building new patterns that root us in our growth.
- **Closure:** A chapter comes to an end. We complete a cycle, whether it's the end of a relationship, a project, a belief system, or even an identity we once clung to. And in that ending, we create space for the next beginning.

It sounds simple on paper, but in practice, most of us get stuck. Not because we're lazy or incapable, but because *our nervous system hates uncertainty.*

Awakening can terrify us. Expansion can overwhelm us. Stability can bore or frustrate us. Closure can feel like a loss we aren't ready to grieve. Each stage demands something different from us, and each one stirs different reactions in the body. Some of us love the rush of new beginnings, but freeze when it's time to act. Others push through the chaos of change but resist slowing down enough to build roots. Some cling to what's familiar long after it's stopped serving them, just because the idea of letting go feels unbearable.

Knowing where we naturally thrive—and where we resist—is vital. It shows us where our ANS might be misfiring. It reveals whether our survival brain is protecting us in ways that no longer make sense for who we are becoming. This isn't about rushing ourselves through the stages. Growth doesn't work that way. It's about paying attention and seeing where our body tenses, where fear clouds our judgment, and where we might be confusing discomfort with danger.

Real change requires an alliance between our mind, our body, and our willingness to endure the vulnerability of transformation. It asks us to reflect on where we get stuck, where we feel safest, and which parts feel most threatening. It also begs us to think about what our nervous system might be trying to protect us from, even if we don't need that protection anymore. When we can name it, we can work with it. We can guide ourselves, gently but firmly, into the next stage. Into the next version of ourselves. Change isn't just something that happens to us. It's something we learn to move through on purpose.

THE BS METER

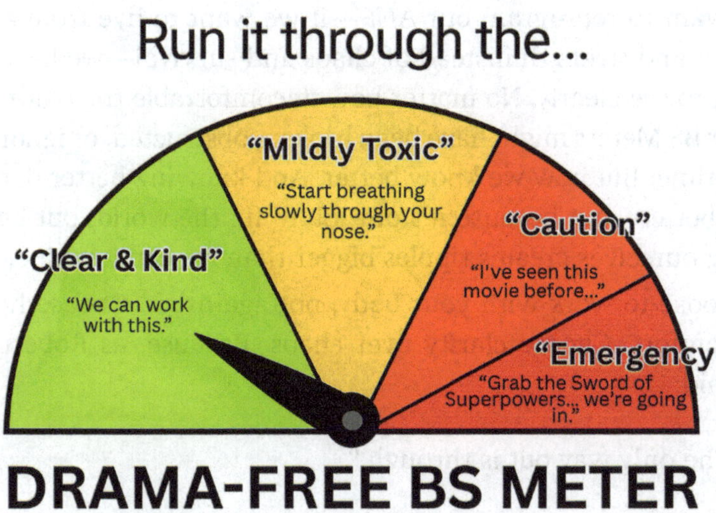

After we get honest about where we tend to land on the Drama Triangle—and where we're stuck in the Anatomy of Change—there's one more tool we need to pull out: the good ol' BS Meter.

Your BS Meter is exactly what it sounds like. It's our internal gauge for separating truth from deception, both in the outside world and within ourselves. It's the tool that keeps us honest when our brain wants to spin a story, rationalize bad habits, or cling to old patterns that feel safer than growth.

For some, a strong BS Meter could mean catching when we're making excuses, avoiding uncomfortable truths, or sugarcoating your behavior. It could be about seeing when our survival instincts are writing checks our reality can't cash, and calling ourselves on it. For others, it's about recognizing when someone's being manipulative, dishonest, or passive-aggressive, and refusing to take things at face value without critical thought. It's the difference between reacting blindly and responding wisely. Think of it like a scale from 1 to 4, and ask yourself:

How close or far am I from seeing the real story?

Owning our denial is a superpower in itself. It's us realizing that if we want to reprogram our ANS—if we want to live from a place of peace and strength instead of chaos and survival—we have to be willing to see clearly. No matter how uncomfortable the truth might be. Our BS Meters might have been broken, obstructed, or ignored for a long time. But now we know better. And knowing better demands we *do* better—not because it's our job to fix the world, but because healing ourselves creates ripples bigger than we can imagine.

Choose to work with your body, not against it. Choose honesty over comfort. Choose clarity over chaos. Because, as Robert Frost once said:

"The only way out is through."

THE ONLY WAY OUT IS THROUGH

Our autonomic nervous system (ANS) is the starting point. It's the seed of everything we feel, believe, and react to. Every time we encounter a stressor, a trigger, or a challenge, our ANS is the first responder. It's deciding, often without our permission, whether we're safe or whether it's time to survive. That's why this work matters so much. Without conscious participation, our bodies just keeps running old codes, pushing us into survival mode even when our lives aren't actually on the line. It's not enough to know that stress happens. We need to know how to move with it differently.

When we notice ourselves getting activated—our heart pounding, our muscles tightening, our brain fogging over—that's our sign that our sympathetic nervous system has taken the wheel. This is our moment to pause. Before we say something we'll regret. Before we make a decision from fear. Before The Drama Triangle pulls us in. And trust me, it will try. The moment we feel threatened, we slip into old survival patterns: victim, persecutor, rescuer. It's automatic. But catching yourself in it? That's where the power lives. We can ask ourselves, without judgment, which role we might be stepping into. Not to shame ourselves or analyze ourselves to death, but to start choosing differently.

It's also important to check where we are in the Anatomy of Change. Change isn't linear. Our nervous system has different reactions to each stage. Sometimes we resist taking the first step. Sometimes we panic midway. Sometimes we cling to the familiar because the ending feels like a free fall. Wherever we find ourselves, just notice it. Our bodies might be reading growth as danger, simply because it's unfamiliar. That's not a reason to stop. It's a reason to slow down and breathe.

That's why the BS Meter is a tool you'll thank yourself for developing. It's easy to mistake familiar feelings for facts. It's easy to believe the stories we've always told ourselves: that we can't change, that it's hopeless, that speaking up will only make it worse. But are those stories actually true, or just well-rehearsed? Our BS Meter helps us reality-check our emotional reactions. It pulls us back into our prefrontal cortex—our center for clear thinking—so we can separate what's real from what's just old survival programming playing on repeat.

Every single one of these tools exists to help us have a different conversation with our bodies. Instead of letting our ANS dictate our reactions, we start actively participating. We start catching ourselves earlier. Calming ourselves faster. Making decisions that aren't just about surviving the moment but about building a life we actually want to live.

The next time your chest tightens, your fists clench, or your mind starts racing toward worst-case scenarios, don't just power through it. Slow down. Listen. Ask yourself:

- What is my body telling me?
- Which survival strategy is trying to take over?
- Where am I in my own process of change?
- Is what I'm believing about this situation actually true?
- And how can I bring myself back to center before I move forward?

This is what working with the ANS looks like in real time. It's not always dramatic. It's not always obvious. But it's everything. Every moment we choose presence over panic, curiosity over reactivity, self-trust over fear, we're doing it. We're changing the system from the inside out. The only way out is through. And we, right now, have everything we need to keep going.

HIGHLIGHT THIS WHOLE SECTION

We can integrate ANS regulation into any situation where we feel our body slipping into fight, flight, or freeze. These are natural mechanisms for managing stress, but without conscious participation, they run the show. One of the simplest, fastest tools I know is the physiological sigh. Dr. Andrew Huberman, a neuroscientist at Stanford, has extensively studied and popularized this practice, showing how it can rapidly calm the nervous system by tapping into the body's natural reflexes.

Originally discovered by Dr. Jack Feldman at UCLA, the physiological sigh is a breathing pattern that occurs naturally during sleep, crying, or heightened emotion. Feldman's early research explored its automatic role, while Huberman's work emphasized how we can use it intentionally to regulate stress. Even 1–3 rounds of this practice can shift the body from heightened anxiety to calm in minutes.

The moment we notice physical signs of stress—tightness, shallow breathing, racing heart—we can use this as a real-time reset. Let's practice:

- Inhale deeply through your nose.
- Take a second, small inhale through your nose to fully expand your lungs.
- Exhale slowly through your mouth until completely empty.

This sequence inflates the alveoli, reduces carbon dioxide buildup, and signals the brain to downshift from stress. It directly activates your parasympathetic nervous system and can restore calm almost immediately. As someone who's lived with anxiety most of my life, I can tell you—this has been one of my most effective tools. And I don't just practice it when I'm anxious. I practice daily, even when I feel fine, conditioning my nervous system so it's ready when I need it. If we only added two minutes a day of physiological sighing, it would be a huge step toward regulating your ANS. It really can be that simple.

Could this have been the farmer's secret in the well-known parable? Maybe. What made him remarkable wasn't luck—it was the way he sustained a down-regulated nervous system. His calm was real, and it was unnerving to those who hadn't yet found their own. In some ways, he is the perfect example of the balance between personal agency and thoughtful comportment. Exactly what we are aiming to achieve within these pages.

Or, perhaps that farmer had another secret. Let's say he used imagery to keep himself calm. Before we roll our eyes and say, "That's a stretch, Eric," hear me out! Studies show that the mere presence or mental image of a loved one can reduce activity in the amygdala and regulate emotional reactivity. According to Polyvagal Theory, cues of safety, like the face or voice of a loved one, can shift the autonomic nervous system from a state of arousal to calm. This happens because the social engagement system processes these cues, overriding the amygdala's fear response. That's why, similarly, imagining social connection activates areas of the brain that inhibit the stress response, quieting the threat circuitry. By engaging the parasympathetic nervous system through visualization of safe connections, one can trigger a calming cascade in the body, helping to regulate heart rate, respiration, and cortisol levels.

I mean, yes, this is all probably a stretch, but tools like the physiological sigh and the power of visualization really do offer simple yet powerful ways to reset our nervous system when stress begins to take hold. They can help us take control over our responses and cultivate a deeper sense of calm that becomes second nature. But, as we've seen, the real change comes from consciously rewiring our emotional and physiological reactions and by recognizing the codes we've built over time and choosing to uncode them. Just like the farmer in the parable, we too can develop a sense of quiet strength that feels unnerving to those who haven't yet learned how to downregulate their own systems. Through this practice, we tap into a true sense of agency, creating lasting change that not only supports our mental well-being but empowers us to live more fully, with intention and presence.

CHAPTER 2:

Activate Safety & Trust – Your Emotional Infrastructure

"Human beings look for safety cues approximately once every 10 seconds."
— Stephen Porges

I remember myself at 13, walking down the hallway of my junior high school next to Julia, my first love. I felt so cool and, to this day, can remember exactly what I was wearing and all of the scenery around me that fateful afternoon.

I knew Julia liked me, too. I could sense it. That is until she stopped and grabbed me by the front of my bony hip, saying emphatically, "Eric, you're too skinny. If you only gained 10 lbs, maybe I'd be your girlfriend, but you're too skinny." She then turned and abruptly walked away as my prepubescent world crumbled.

I went from feeling like the king of junior high to being hit with a sledgehammer in my stomach. I thought I might throw up. A psychotherapist would say in that moment I disassociated. I left my body. It was all too much to handle, and I can still recall how I felt walking around in a daze for a while after. Less than ten seconds; that's all it took for her words to flip my 13-year-old world around.

I vividly remember being in the shower that evening, still feeling down and out. When I looked in the mirror after, for the first time, I saw "lack." Before that day, I saw myself as a 13-year-old, brilliant, young human being. But at that moment, she took an arrow and shot it deep into me. I cried, thinking I was unattractive and too skinny. That record played over and over again in my mind.

Again, less than ten seconds was all it took for her words to make my world crumble. Little did I know it would take ten years to unwind the piercing effects of those few painful seconds.

It wasn't until therapy in my 20s because some other woman broke my heart that my well-meaning therapist said, "You may have some body issues that developed somewhere in your history, Eric."

I looked at her with a face of denial. "Who? Me? I don't have body issues." With her help, my brain started peeling back the layers of my experiences to that point. That comment Julia made impacted my clothes, my confidence level, and everything about the way I presented myself. And I carried that dialogue in my mind, all roads leading to that little interaction of my childhood.

"Oh, wow. I do have body image issues," I said to her. Remember that coding process of the ANS? Yeah, well, at that moment, I did some heavy coding.

As I began the inner work to release some of the negative codes associated with my body after that incident, I came across this piece of research by Margaret Kemeny where she says that in a review of over 200 studies examining stress and cortisol, being negatively evaluated—especially by someone of importance or interest to you—is the most important variable that elevates cortisol in our blood during a stressful event.

This made a lot of sense to me. Julia was definitely important; possibly the most important peer I had at that time. Her judgment of me created trauma that I stored in my body for a long time, and the stress of it rippled onto numerous parts of my life. It dismantled my psychological safety and trust, all from one negative evaluation.

Before I unravel this, I want to offer up the way in which I define safety and trust, and the context in which it will be discussed in this chapter.

- Safety is the feeling of being secure and protected—in your body or environment—free to express yourself without fear of judgment or harm.
- Trust is the belief in your own and others' integrity and compassion; that your presence and voice are valued.

Together, safety and trust form the foundation to show up fully and authentically without fear of backlash or drama.

WHY WE NEED TO FEEL PSYCHOLOGICALLY SAFE TO THRIVE

To understand safety and trust, it helps to define what it looks like when they are present—in teams, relationships, and within ourselves. In my years of coaching wellness professionals and teaching team collaboration, psychological safety is the concept that consistently blows people's minds. They often treat it like a secret key to high-functioning teams. But it's not a secret.

In 2012, Google launched Project Aristotle to answer one question: *What makes a team successful?* The project's name nodded to Aristotle's claim that *"The whole is greater than the sum of its parts."* After extensive research, they landed on one unexpected, central finding: psychological safety.

Harvard professor Amy Edmondson, a lead researcher on the project, defined psychological safety as *"a shared belief held by members of a team that the team is safe for interpersonal risk-taking."* It's an environment built on trust and respect, where people can be themselves, speak up, ask questions, and admit mistakes without fear of judgment or punishment.

Google found that team success wasn't about intelligence, skill level, or background—it was about how safe people felt. The highest-performing teams had high levels of trust, dependability, and clearly defined goals. People worked better not because they were better, but because they felt safe to show up fully.

Motivational speaker and leadership expert Simon Sinek expands on this in his TED Talk *Why Good Leaders Make You Feel Safe.* He describes a "circle of safety," an adaptive system humans evolved to create in order to survive together. Inside this circle, people protect each other from external threats. But what about when the circle breaks down?

"If the conditions are wrong," Sinek says, "we're forced to expend our own time and energy to protect ourselves from each other. And that inherently weakens the organization."

Sound familiar? How many of us are burning energy protecting ourselves from people we *should* be collaborating with? How many times have we wanted to say, "The conditions are wrong here," but didn't feel safe enough to speak?

This isn't just a workplace problem—it's everywhere. Whether it's a friend group, a family, a romantic relationship, or a creative community, we all want the same thing: to belong without fear of being judged, shamed, or excluded. We want to be in a space where we can simply *be.*

But fear has taken the lead. We fear layoffs, AI, breakups, rejection, irrelevance, loneliness, and not achieving what we "should." So we overcompensate—losing sleep, skipping meals, snapping at loved ones—feeding the drama loop. We're too scared to be vulnerable, so we stay stuck. Judgment becomes the default. Disconnection follows.

Despite all our digital "connections," we're more isolated than ever. And I believe judgment—whether we give it or receive it—is at the core. As Dr. JP Pawliw-Fry says, judgment is *corrosive* to our being. It undermines our humanity. And once we feel unsafe, trust evaporates.

"Oh hell no, you're not going to hurt me again." That was me after Julia's comment about my body. I changed how I dressed and carried myself, not out of empowerment, but fear. I didn't want to feel that pain again. Porges' Polyvagal Theory explains that our ability to experience arousal or rest depends on whether fear is present. We can only truly relax when we feel safe. But when we're always bracing for judgment, even rest becomes impossible. Let's break it down:

Judgment = Lack of Safety = Distrust = Drama = Stress = Negative Outcomes = Emotional Cost

It's a cycle we live in until we create the conditions to step out of it. We can't stop external chaos, but we can control how we show up. We can create inner and relational safety starting with ourselves. We can become the kind of people who keep the circle intact.

HOW JUDGMENT CORRODES OUR SAFETY NET

One of the most damaging forces in our relationship with ourselves and others is judgment, especially the kind that devalues. Judgment strips us of internal safety. It tells us we aren't enough and trains us to distrust ourselves. When our self-worth is threatened, the parasympathetic nervous system—the part that calms and soothes—is blocked. That moment with Julia? None of it felt safe. Once I no longer felt safe in my body, I became an unreliable narrator of my own experience.

Dr. JP Pawliw-Fry, in *Is Stress Working For You or Against You?*, describes two major mental traps:

> "The corrosive nature of judgment and the brain's inability to distinguish what's real from what's imagined."

Julia's words became the root of a warped self-image. My 13-year-old brain couldn't separate fact from perception. Her projection felt like the truth: I wasn't attractive. Shame set in, and the guilt followed for not living up to who I thought I was. I internalized judgment as a personal flaw instead of situational noise. I became hyper-aware of how others saw me, afraid someone else would say what she did. That's chronic stress. Why? Because, as Margaret Kemeny reminds us, social judgment floods the body with cortisol.

Additional research shows our brains process social pain the same way we process physical pain. I felt it in my stomach, my breath, my heart rate. But the deeper harm was how judgment shut down my self-empathy. Over time, it became the background music of my life—a low hum of not-enoughness. My nervous system adapted to the stress and made it my baseline. And when we're constantly reacting to outside threats—like judgment—we lose the energy to repair our internal world.

That's exactly how I developed a Fixed Invisible Belief (or FIB), which, according to Pawliw-Fry is a deeply embedded, often unconscious belief about ourselves that resists change even when proven wrong. FIBs keep us locked into outdated truths and false limits. Mine was that I was "too skinny to be lovable or worthy." I didn't realize it, but that belief made me self-sabotage. I drifted from my authentic self.

We all carry unspoken beliefs about who we are and what we deserve. Most were formed early, sometimes from just a single sentence or moment that caught us off guard and embedded itself in our nervous system. These are our FIBs, the subconscious stories that quietly direct our behavior, our relationships, and our sense of self-worth. They are often invisible, but they feel true. And until we examine them, they tend to run the show.

Some common FIBs include:

- "I'm a burden."
- "I have to earn love."
- "People always leave."
- "If I don't perform, I'll be abandoned."
- "I can't trust anyone with the real me."

These beliefs are usually installed without our awareness and accepted as fact. But the truth is: they are stories, not identities.

FIBs make us more susceptible to judgment. We take it personally instead of as an opportunity for growth. And while the story about Julia began at 13, it was only one example in a lifetime of judgment chipping away at my inner foundation.

Most of us carry a "thorn" in our sides—a moment, a comment, a judgment—that wasn't ours to bear, but pierced us deeply. Often it came from someone important. And often, it first happened in childhood, leaving a wound that makes us bleed. Maybe it's a boss who shuts down your voice in meetings. A partner who dismissed our dreams. A family member whose opinions silence us. Whatever it is, it leaves us feeling vulnerable. Unsafe. We don't feel grounded in our bodies because we're anticipating being judged, rejected, or misunderstood.

This hypervigilance—whether conscious or not—keeps our nervous system flooded with cortisol. It blocks presence, ease, and authenticity. So here's what I want us to consider:

> What is my thorn? What is the story I tell myself because of that thorn, and what belief was born from that moment?

The thorn is often small and is lodged from just a sentence, a glance, or a gesture. But it is mighty and lodges deep. And because it came from someone we trusted, admired, or loved, it bypasses our logic centers and heads straight for the emotional brain. In neuroscience terms, that's the limbic system, especially the amygdala.

When we feel judged, rejected, or shamed (especially in formative years), the brain encodes that moment with a heightened surge of cortisol and adrenaline. Our autonomic nervous system takes a snapshot. It says: *This freaking hurt. Don't let it happen again.* That single moment becomes a neural landmark that anchors as a conditioned response, which gets replayed every time a similar situation arises.

That's how a thorn becomes more than a memory. It becomes a pattern.

Over time, the thorn can help shape our default mode network—the part of the brain active when we're daydreaming or self-reflecting. If left unhealed, it colors our self-perception, wiring in a loop of "not enoughness." We begin to form FIBs not just emotionally, but neurologically. It's not just a story we tell; it's a pathway our brain reinforces, again and again.

Here's the paradox of the thorn: we didn't choose it, but we often build our lives around it. We dress around it. We date around it. We speak, work, and dream around it. All to avoid brushing up against that old wound again. But avoidance doesn't rewire anything—it only deepens the groove.

If only avoidance would heal it... but it doesn't.

Healing, from a brain-based perspective, comes through neuroplasticity—our innate ability to change the brain by changing our thoughts, behaviors, and emotional responses. This happens when we:

- Name the thorn
- Reframe the story it told us
- Practice new responses that signal safety to the nervous system

And most of all, when we stop giving the thorn the final say. The thorn wasn't our fault. But the story it grew into? That's now ours to rewrite.

SAFETY IS A BIOLOGICALLY-DRIVEN NEED

Safety is a biological imperative. Our nervous system constantly scans for safety cues, roughly every ten seconds according to Stephen Porges, the neuroscientist known for the Polyvagal Theory we discussed in the last chapter. This instinct is rooted in our autonomic nervous system, especially the ventral vagal complex, the branch of the vagus nerve responsible for emotional regulation, social engagement, and our ability to rest and digest.

Porges's Polyvagal Theory shows us that safety is just as much physiological as it is psychological. It's felt in the body through neural feedback loops between the brain and internal organs. When the ventral vagus is active, we're calm, connected, and capable of being our authentic selves. When it's underactive, we struggle with anxiety, reactivity, and stress overload.

Despite "survival of the fittest" narratives, human survival depends on connection. The ventral vagus plays a central role in these social behaviors, regulating facial expressions, vocal tone, and engagement cues that build trust and help us detect safety in others.

When we feel safe, our BS Meters work. We discern what's helpful, connect without drama, and stay grounded. In this state, our resources are used for healing and growth, not defense. But when we're stuck in a fight-or-flight state, the body can't repair itself. It's too busy bracing for the next perceived threat.

These patterns begin in infancy. How we're soothed, held, and responded to shapes our ability to self-regulate later in life. For those with trauma histories, the nervous system can become locked in defense mode. Social connection feels unsafe, and dissociation becomes a coping mechanism. In these states, the autonomic nervous system is dysregulated, often affecting our mental health, stress levels, and capacity for connection.

My own unresolved wounds resurfaced in my twenties, when a man I barely knew in a hot tub casually said, "You're a good-looking guy. You should lift weights to build your chest."

WTH?!

Once again, a body judgment was tossed at me, unsolicited. I'd always been self-conscious shirtless, often keeping my shirt on at pools and beaches. That day, I was already on edge, even if I didn't realize it. His comment activated my nervous system, not just in that moment, but through the lens of every past experience that told me my body wasn't enough. The thorn in my side started to bleed out into the water.

The irony was that he didn't even have a muscular chest. He didn't seem confident. But projection doesn't need logic. He freely unloaded his insecurities onto me, and my body, trained to see danger in judgment, responded with stress, shame, and a rush of old narratives.

That's the Polyvagal Theory in action. Our bodies remember. They track every insult, rejection, or jab and store it. Unless we interrupt that loop, our systems stay in high alert.

HERE'S WHY WE DON'T FEEL SAFE

I've asked myself: How can we feel safe in a world more concerned with appearances than authenticity? We're all bracing for judgment, often without realizing it. We don't want to seem weak, wrong, or different. So, we take 67 selfies to post one. We may pursue careers we don't really want. We downplay our quirks, hide our flaws, and silence our truth. Because judgment = danger. And many of us already feel unsafe in our bodies. I know I often do.

Warren Buffett once posed a question:

> "If you could learn something valuable but it would make you look bad, would you do it?"

Often, the answer is no because we fear looking foolish more than we fear staying stuck. There are so few spaces in our lives where we feel safe enough to take a risk and be ourselves. But here's the truth: safety isn't just the absence of threat. It's the presence of stability where we aren't trapped in chronic shame, fear, or hypervigilance.

I could've cut Julia out of my life entirely after that day. I could've changed schools, states, everything. But it wouldn't have mattered. The next Julia would've shown up anyway. Until I rewired the story in my nervous system, the threat would always feel real. This is a crucial point. There is always another to twist the thorn.

When we live in a state of unsafety, our body prioritizes survival over healing. We can't grow, restore, or connect because the sympathetic nervous system is stuck in overdrive. It blocks our ability to access calm, grounded states through the ventral vagus. That's why presence is so hard. Without safety and trust, we can't truly be here. We isolate. We censor ourselves. We become creatively blocked. And in a culture addicted to external validation, it's even harder to explore our internal world.

And yet—we're all participating. We're all judging while fearing judgment. We all know stress is killing us. But we either don't have the tools, or we don't feel safe enough to use them. Judge or be judged, right? Wrong. But it's still the path most of us take.

Feeling unsafe means we stop trusting not just the environment, but ourselves. We hesitate to speak up, take initiative, or express creativity. We lean into performance and perfectionism. We measure worth in likes, promotions, and approval, feeding a cycle of disconnection. But we don't have to keep playing that game.

We get to say: "I'm done performing. I'm done shrinking. I want to feel safe and true in my own skin."

Go back to the thorn in your side. Ask:

- Who could I become if I finally let it go? Don't just imagine it—feel it.
- What shifts in my body when I no longer carry that fear or pain? What becomes possible?

Some may be wondering what happened when I saw Julia again...

At our 30-year high school reunion, she pulled up a stool next to me at the bar. After some small talk about life—jobs, kids, divorces—she stopped and pointed at my forehead.

"What are those lines on your forehead?"

For a moment, I was stunned. Then I felt something unexpected: empathy. I saw a 13-year-old girl trapped in a 50-year-old body, still battling her inner critic. Still projecting. Still looking for safety in control and critique.

I smiled and said, "They're just wrinkles—I *am* 50, after all." Then I lifted my drink, wished her well, and disappeared into the crowd, quietly proud of who I'd become. She hadn't changed. But I had. Her judgment no longer held power over me. She couldn't pierce my sense of safety or distort my self-trust. Because this time, I had done the work.

The reason we don't feel safe often lies in the judgments we've internalized from others—and from ourselves. We've been conditioned to hide, perform, and seek approval, believing that vulnerability equals danger. The fear of judgment keeps us stuck in cycles of self-protection and perfectionism, blocking our ability to truly connect or grow. To shift this, we need to identify our own "Julia"—the person or moment that has shaped our fear and made us feel unsafe.

Take a moment now to reflect:

- Who was your "Julia"?
- What did they say (or not say) that pierced your sense of safety?
- What belief took root because of that moment?

By acknowledging who or what has held power over our sense of safety, we can begin to untangle those beliefs, rewire the story we've been telling ourselves, and create a new narrative rooted in self-trust and authenticity. This is the key to stepping out of the cycle of judgment and into a life where we feel secure enough to show up as our true selves.

WIELD YOUR SWORD OF SUPERPOWERS

Taking Porges's theory into account, one of the most powerful things we can do for ourselves is to separate our feelings from the behaviors and thoughts attached to them. Feelings are part of an adaptive system; they aren't always logical or under our conscious control. But when we feel psychologically safe, we gain the capacity to pause, to reflect, and to break the habitual chain between fear, judgment, and reaction.

We are not our thoughts. We are not our behaviors. We are conscious beings navigating the complex terrain of emotions, patterns, and experiences. And in that process, we're allowed to pause before reacting, to listen before judging, to respond with both courage and care.

This is where the Sword of Superpowers comes in.

When it comes to safety and trust, the sword will help us form the foundation for unconditional positive regard—and for the type of kindness we are promoting throughout this book. Unconditional positive regard is a concept coined by Carl Rogers in the 1960s. It involves accepting and supporting a person (or ourselves) without judgment, regardless of the associated thoughts, feelings, or behaviors that might arise. As a psychologist, Rogers brought this concept to therapists to use with their clients, helping them practice non-judgment and compassion on their healing journey. He says caring for a client means accepting all of the client's thoughts, feelings, and behaviors without any conditions attached to that acceptance." This is also an invitation for us to accept ourselves (and others) without conditions or judgment.

We often think we're only worthy when we meet certain standards—when we behave the "right" way, say the "right" thing, look the "right" way. But the truth is: our worth is not conditional. And when we forget that, we remain in survival mode, reinforcing the drama we say we want to escape. Ask yourself:

> What is my role in the success or dysfunction of my own psychological safety?

That's our sword-in-the-ground moment. That's our call to pause, to reflect, and to reclaim our power. When we trust ourselves enough to hold the sword with clarity and compassion, we become a safer space, not only for ourselves but for everyone around us.

A WORD ON BOUNDARIES AND SAFETY

Someone who truly understands their worth does not easily absorb external judgment. They have boundaries, forged from self-awareness and shaped by compassion, not fear.

Brené Brown reminds us that:

> "Compassionate people ask for what they need. They say no when they need to, and when they say yes, they mean it. They're compassionate because their boundaries keep them out of resentment."

Why? Because compassion without clarity is enabling. And clarity without compassion is just cruelty in disguise.

Drama often enters our lives as a breach of agreement—someone crosses a boundary we didn't enforce, or we ignored our internal signals until it hurt. But when we wield our sword, we learn to cut through the noise and say, "This is not okay," without armor, without malice.

I think back to a moment during a workshop I was leading. A participant made a sexually inappropriate comment. Without hesitation, I stood up and said clearly, "If you or anyone else makes an inappropriate comment in this room, I will personally escort you out. Am I clear?"

Silence.

But also—a shift.

Afterward, someone came up to me and said, "I don't know what you just did, but it was powerful."

It wasn't just the sword—it was the boundary, backed by empathy, accountability, and resilience (EAR). I didn't shame the person, but I didn't coddle them either. I protected the space with firm compassion. That's what the sword is for. That's what psychological safety requires.

We're not meant to walk around cutting people's heads off emotionally. But we're also not meant to dull ourselves down into passive silence. Many of us have done both. We've wielded the sword too harshly or not at all. We've turned it inward with judgment or outward with aggression. Neither serves us.

Boundaries are the healthy middle path. They tell the truth with love. They protect the parts of us that are sacred and help others rise to meet us in that respect. They are how we say, "I value myself, and I value you enough to be clear."

But let's be honest: setting boundaries often triggers discomfort. It challenges our deepest fears—of rejection, of being seen as "too much," of losing love. That's where the EAR framework comes back in:

- **Empathy** says, "It's okay to feel afraid right now. This fear makes sense."
- **Accountability** says, "But I'm still choosing to honor what's true for me."
- **Resilience** says, "Even if this boundary isn't received well, I can handle the discomfort—and I'll still be okay."

So I'll ask this: Do you believe you're worthy of safety and trust?

Not just in theory, but in practice. Even when upholding that worth disappoints others. Even when it's messy. Even when we don't get applause. The sword is already in our hands. The question is: Will we learn to use it wisely?

Because the goal isn't perfection, it's alignment. And when we wield the Sword of Superpowers with empathy, accountability, and resilience at our side, we stop fearing conflict. We stop over-accommodating. We stop shrinking. We become someone who can say a fierce "no" from a place of deep, unwavering love.

TRUSTING YOURSELF TO RECONSTRUCT YOUR SAFETY NET

Before we wrap up, let's take a moment to summarize the key insights we've explored in this chapter:

- Judgment corrodes the nature of our being and diminishes our ability to feel safe in our bodies or environment.

- Safety is a biologically driven need, rooted in our nervous system, that shapes our behaviors, emotions, and social interactions.
- We don't feel safe because we prioritize external validation over internal processing, leaving us trapped in cycles of judgment, fear, and disconnection that hinder our ability to trust ourselves and heal.
- Without trust and a sense of safety, we expend energy protecting ourselves rather than collaborating and being present.
- True psychological safety stems from unconditional self-acceptance, allowing us to separate our worth from our thoughts and actions.
- Recognizing our inherent worth empowers us to establish and uphold boundaries that ensure our well-being while navigating the complexities of life.

Drama is created when we operate from a place of fear, insecurity, and judgment. When we don't feel safe in our bodies or our environment, we become reactive, defensive, and overly reliant on external validation, which fuels a cycle of stress and disconnection. If we do not trust that we are safe, we will see everything as a threat.

So, if the autonomic nervous system is the seed, then safety and trust are the roots that offer us the stability we need to grow that seed. It's the next thing we must give our undivided attention to before we can sprout. We cannot become a fruit-bearing tree without well-nurtured roots. It's just not possible. This means having a safe place to grow. It means trusting in our environment to do what's best for that growth process—and removing ourselves from environments that don't.

While we can't always predict when we'll be in situations or around people who make us feel unsafe, we can take small steps to create a sense of safety within ourselves—whether that's by identifying our boundaries, listening to our gut feelings, or reminding ourselves that we don't need external permission to protect our well-being. We can trust ourselves enough to know we've got it covered. When we trust ourselves, we create a protective barrier against external judgment and manipulation, enabling us to establish and maintain healthy boundaries that keep us safe. We shift our focus inward and prioritize our self-perception over others' opinions. Our BS Meters are plugged in, and we are consciously assessing what environments, people, or things support our safety or undermine it.

When I say "trust that we have it covered," I mean trust that we can regulate our system when it's starting to feel unsafe. I mean that we are in tune with the bodily cues that are telling us we're on high alert or hyper-aroused or require a breather. It means we know the definition of safety for us and how to maintain it—no exceptions. It doesn't happen overnight, but we can start small and deepen our practice over time until it feels like second nature.

In addition to the physiological sigh I mentioned in the last chapter, another of my favorite ways to reduce amygdala activity and engage the parasympathetic nervous system is the intentional practice of rapid eye movement (REM). While most people REM with the sleep stage where dreams occur, intentional eye movement has also been explored as a tool for reducing stress and processing emotions while awake. Neuroscientist Dr. Andrew Huberman and other researchers suggest that moving our eyes from side to side can help shift the nervous system out of a stress response by engaging brain circuits responsible for emotional regulation. Studies indicate that bilateral eye movement may decrease activity in the amygdala, the brain's fear-processing center, leading to a calmer state.

This practice is also a core component of Eye Movement Desensitization and Reprocessing (EMDR) therapy, developed by psychologist Francine Shapiro in the late 1980s. EMDR is widely recognized for its effectiveness in treating trauma and anxiety, using guided eye movements to help the brain reprocess distressing experiences. Some researchers propose that EMDR may share neural mechanisms with REM sleep, where the brain naturally consolidates emotional memories.

Beyond clinical therapy, incorporating intentional lateral eye movements into daily routines may help regulate stress, promote emotional resilience, and enhance cognitive flexibility. By reducing reactivity, the brain becomes better equipped to make clear, drama-free decisions. While more research is needed to fully understand the broader applications, simple exercises like shifting your gaze side to side for 30–60 seconds may serve as a quick reset for the nervous system.

Here's how to practice Bilateral Eye Movement for emotional reset:

- **Get Comfortable:** Find a comfortable place to sit or stand for a minute where you won't be disturbed. Let your spine stay straight but relaxed, and as much as possible, keep your head held still without moving.
- **Choose a Reference Point:** You can use any stimulus: your finger, a pen, or any small object about 12–16 inches in front of your face. Or if you prefer, simply pick two fixed points in your environment to practice with (e.g., two objects at eye level on either side of a room).
- **Move Your Eyes Side to Side:** If using your finger or an object, slowly move it from left to right, ensuring your eyes follow it smoothly. Keep your head still and allow only your eyes to move. If using fixed points, shift your gaze back and forth between them.
- **Find Your Own Comfortable Rhythm:** Move your eyes from left to right at a steady pace (not too fast or too slow). A typical speed is one full left-right cycle per second (similar to a metronome at 60 beats per minute). Continue for 30–60 seconds or until you notice a sense of relaxation.
- **Observe Sensations:** Take note of how you feel after a short practice. Pay close attention to any shifts in your breathing

and heart rate. Many people report experiencing reduced mental chatter and a sense of calm.

- **Repeat as Needed:** Lather, rinse, repeat. You can ideally set a goal to practice this 1-3 times a day, especially during acute moments of stress or emotional overwhelm.

Try it a few times a week and notice the feelings that arise.

As we continue to dismantle the stigmas surrounding self-care, this simple practice reminds us that taking care of our mental and emotional well-being doesn't have to be complicated. Ultimately, we want to develop a habit of simple, evidence-based practices that can be done in real time to downregulate our ANS.

CHAPTER 3:

Activate Your Vision and Values - Letting Passion Guide You

"If you bring forth what is within you, what you bring forth will save you. If you do not bring forth what is within you, what you do not bring forth will destroy you."

— Gospel of Thomas- Verse 70

Prince wasn't just an artist writing songs. He was continually bringing forth something from the deepest parts of himself. In 1983, within the purple-lit corridors of his creative sanctum, he pieced together the bones of a ballad unlike anything he had ever written. It was grand, emotional, and filled with an aching sense of longing. But something was missing. The lyrics! The magic…

Enter Stevie Nicks. She played in the realm of magic.

Prince adored her, and the respect was mutual. She was the reigning enchantress of Rock and Roll, a poetess who could weave entire worlds with a whisper. If anyone could crack the code of this aching melody, it was her. He handed her the demo—just music, no lyrics—and invited her to see if the music moved her to compose.

She pressed play.

As the song unfolded, swelling with the weight of something vast and cinematic, she felt something unexpected: *intimidation*. The melody was too big. Too powerful. It sounded like the climax of a movie that hadn't been written yet. The emotions it stirred were too profound to be captured in words—not hers, anyway.

She called Prince back: "I can't do it. It's too much. This is all yours." The song had found its true owner.

And so, the song returned home. Prince sat down, took back the wheel, and patiently let it take shape. *Purple Rain* wasn't meant to be written by anyone else. It had always been his story to tell. His vision.

By the time he finished, it had transformed into a sweeping, gospel-tinged epic- part love song, part farewell, part spiritual awakening. A song that felt like the end of the world and the beginning of another. When he played it for his band, The Revolution, it was clear: this wasn't just another song. This was something immortal. And we could argue this one song shaped the trajectory of the rest of his career.

Sometimes, the greatest gifts are the ones returned to us. Similarly, another epic music classic went through a similar vision quest…

Mike Campbell was no stranger to magic. As Tom Petty's right-hand man and guitar sorcerer for the Heartbreakers, he had a way of pulling melodies from the ether and turning them into gold. One day, in the early '80s, he stumbled upon something different. A hypnotic, arpeggiated, driving riff. It felt like headlights on an empty highway, like summer fading into memory. He laid it down on a four-track cassette and brought it straight to Tom.

Petty listened and immediately felt it. But he also knew one thing: it wasn't right for *Southern Accents*, the sprawling concept album he was shaping at the time. It wasn't that the song wasn't good, but just like Stevie Nicks concluded, it just wasn't *his* song.

So, Campbell took a shot in the dark. He handed the demo to Don Henley, the golden voice of the Eagles. Henley, fresh off the Eagles' implosion, was looking for something new, something that sounded like tomorrow. When he pressed play, he felt it in a way Petty hadn't. The music already spoke directly to him; all it needed was the right words. And within hours of hearing the demo, he penned the seminal words:

"Nobody on the road, nobody on the beach⊠"

Henley later called it "the greatest song he's ever written." Parts of the song give me goosebumps. It is a nostalgic tale of aging, regret, and longing wrapped in shimmering synths, a love song to summers that never return. It became a defining anthem of the 1980s and beyond. The song still echoes across beaches, highways, and open windows all over the world. The third verse continues:

"Out of the road today, I saw a Deadhead sticker on a Cadillac".

(Side note: IMHO, this is one of the greatest, singular lines in the history of Rock and Roll.)

As for Petty? He never sweated it. He and Campbell had their own anthems to write. In the end, the song ended up exactly where it was supposed to be.

Prince had a masterpiece in his hands, but at first, he tried to hand it off to someone else. Mike Campbell wrote the music to one of the greatest rock songs of all time, but it wasn't meant for the person he originally gave it to. Both songs had to find their rightful place in the world, just as we must align our lives with who we truly are. We shouldn't shape ourselves based on who we've been told we should be, nor force ourselves into a song that isn't meant for us just because someone else says it is.

Too many of us are living lives built around *roles*—jobs, titles, companies—rather than *visions*. We chase the career, the paycheck, the promotion, thinking that if we just get the right title, everything else will fall into place. But more often than not, it doesn't. Instead, it consumes us.

We get caught up in this cycle, climbing the ladder, thinking that once we reach the top, we'll finally be able to breathe and enjoy life. But the reality is, we often don't stop to take a breath, and the life we imagine for ourselves—one filled with purpose and authenticity—remains just out of reach. We tell ourselves, "Once I get the promotion, the approval, the recognition, then I'll be able to live the life I've dreamed of." But, like Prince and Tom Petty, we may spend years handing off our dreams and talents to fit someone else's expectations, or worse, surrender to the idea that the life we want is not meant for us. The truth is, just like the songs that found their rightful place, we must align our lives with who we truly are, not who we've been told to be. The pursuit of external validation can consume us if we let it, but if we take a step back and reconnect with our vision—our true song—we can stop performing and start living.

What I'm proposing is that instead of designing our lives around a job, we can design our job around our lives. We can sing our own song. It is possible. We just have to be willing to flip the script, edit the lyrics, and start with what we truly want to sing about—our vision, our values, our passions—and then find work that fits into that.

Prince could have forced *Purple Rain* into someone else's hands, and it would have been a very different song—or maybe no song at all. Mike Campbell could have buried that demo when Petty passed on it, but instead, he let it find the right voice.

The same is true for us. If we don't bring forth what is within us—our values, our vision, our purpose—we risk being swallowed by a life that isn't truly ours.

So, ask yourself:

- Am I shaping my life around a job, or am I shaping my job around the life I want?
- Am I living according to values that are truly mine or ones that were handed to me?
- If what I'm doing doesn't light me up, is it because I'm out of alignment with what really matters to me?

The answer isn't to force something that doesn't fit. The answer is to step back, realign, and bring forth what is truly within. Because what we don't bring forth—the vision that remains buried, the values left unexamined—has the power to dismantle us.

WHAT IS WITHIN YOU?

Just like those epic songs, our life's purpose is waiting for the right voice. Our authenticity *is* the right voice. Designing our life is analogous to composing a brilliant piece of music, similar to the yellow-brick road Prince, Mike Campbell, and Don Henley traversed.

And it all begins with our vision.

To this point, we've been talking a lot about the body. After all, our body is the seed, the starting point of this life cycle we're in. The rest is essentially useless without a keen understanding of the system that manages and regulates that growth cycle.

We've discussed so far that consciously learning to manage and regulate our ANS allows us to control our responses to life's challenges. We explored how trauma and judgment disrupt the connection between the mind and body, breaking down the sense of safety and trust needed for them to work in harmony.

Safety and trust are the root system, the aspects of our lives that provide stability and nourishment to our ever-changing seed. Without these two elements in place, the mind and body become estranged, operating independently and often at odds with one another. Without safety and trust, drama and chaos continue to unfold, costing us peace, clarity, and growth.

For those who have made it this far, we're likely reflecting on how life shaped our current paths and where our sense of safety fractured, where trust got lost, and where external noise pulled us out of alignment. Some may be saying, "Wow! Eric! You're right! My system's dysregulated. I don't trust myself with certain people, things, or situations. I don't feel safe in my body. I remember that time as a kid when..."

We might be reeling through all the experiences in our lives that have led us to this point. There's a chance some are delving deeper into our history, into uncovering with curiosity the people, places, and events that have shaped us, asking:

> Where did I get caught up in all the external noise instead of working with my system to bring forth what is within me?

The fact is, we've all got noise. Let's normalize its existence. As we move through this chapter, notice if the perfectionist shows its head. Identify that as noise as well. This work often involves a lengthy, introspective process as it invites deep change, often with very deeply held beliefs that may be difficult to let go of. Only we can decide how to sift through the noise and all the questions that come with it. None of us are alone, and I will offer strong insight to track where we are and how we might look to find the answers.

The reason I avoid telling people exactly how to change their lives is because I don't know what real, meaningful change means for them. I don't know what's beyond their noise. I only know what's beyond mine. On any given day, I could fill a chapter with my own noise and drama and BS, but that wouldn't necessarily help anyone find their truth or navigate their journey.

As a coach, I have witnessed firsthand the wisdom shared in one of my favorite quotes by Rainer Maria Rilke:

> "Be patient toward all that is unsolved in your heart and try to love the questions themselves, like locked rooms and like books that are now written in a very foreign tongue. Do not now seek the answers, which cannot be given to you because you would not be able to live them. And the point is, to live everything. Live the questions now. Perhaps you will then gradually, without noticing it, live along some distant day into the answer."

In the spirit of Rilke, this chapter will ask many questions of us. Some questions may have immediate answers, but many will stay with us for days, weeks, or even months, until we grow into them.

This is the chapter where we get in touch. I'll ask questions that get to the heart of who we are, why we are here, and what is important to us. It is going to require deep reflection, and for us to be an active participant instead of just a reader and absorber of this information.

WHAT'S THE DRIVING FORCE?

As we explored in Chapter One, when the nervous system is dysregulated, our sense of clarity gets hijacked. This chapter builds on that by showing how to restore that clarity through value-based visioning. My work is about helping people bridge the mind-body gap—the disconnect between what we think we want and what we truly feel and value. When that gap closes, we begin to move differently. We begin to make decisions that align with who we are at our core. But once we cross that bridge, the next question is: Where are we going?

Every day, we make tens of thousands of conscious choices—some research estimates around 35,000. And yet, most of us make those decisions without a clear sense of direction. We follow templates handed to us by family, school, culture, capitalism—paths designed to appear successful or validated. But at some point, many of us stop and ask: "Whose life am I actually living?" Is it yours? Or one designed by an outside system or someone else?

If you're reading this, I know you're not here to survive on autopilot. You're here to do something different, to stop fighting the current and start riding the wave. Me too. As Alan Watts once wrote:

> "The meaning of life is just to be alive. It is so plain and so obvious and so simple. And yet, everybody rushes around in a great panic as if it were necessary to achieve something beyond themselves."

The panic starts the moment we seek fulfillment outside ourselves. When we chase someone else's version of a successful life, creativity stalls, self-expression dims, and we get stuck in loops of stress, confusion, and drama. We're going nowhere fast—not because we're broken, but because we never paused to ask where we actually want to go.

To begin clarifying that, imagine something far beyond the noise.

I want each of us to picture our arrival into the afterlife, whatever that means to us. For me, I'm greeted by my father (my hero), and after a long-overdue reunion and a perfect cup of coffee, I'm handed a plush robe by a spa attendant and escorted to a massage table where I receive a foot massage for as long as I want.

Who's there? What's happening? Why does it feel so good? When visualizing this version of peace, our core values are revealed. Without sitting with our vision and assessing what we value, we chase goals we don't care about, make decisions that drain us, and stay in jobs, relationships, or environments that suffocate us. We suffer not because we're weak, but because we're misaligned.

Some of us may already feel this—conflicted, uncertain, overwhelmed. Decision-making feels impossible. But as Moshe Feldenkrais said:

> "You can't change what you're doing until you know what you're doing."

So, let's look at what the driving force is. Because whatever it is—conscious or unconscious—it's shaping our entire lives. Most people fall into one of two camps when it comes to life orientation:

- **Job or Position as Driving Force:** They work primarily for status, security, income, or advancement. Their job takes up most of their energy and becomes the centerpiece of their identity.
- **Lifestyle as Driving Force:** They design their work around the life they want to live. Work is part of a larger mosaic—family, freedom, hobbies, health, relationships—and doesn't dominate the picture.

Neither is right nor wrong, but knowing which one truly resonates with us is critical. Statistically, most people are disengaged at work. A Gallup survey found that 70% of Americans feel disconnected from their jobs, and of those, nearly 30% are actively disengaged—meaning they're not just unfulfilled, they're checked out. Nearly half of working adults admit they only work out of necessity, not passion.

This chronic dissatisfaction bleeds into everything—stress, health problems, sleep issues, strained relationships, even heart attacks, most of which occur on Monday mornings. That's not just bad luck. It's systemic misalignment.

We've been trained to choose a job, title, or income bracket first and build a life around that. But what if we flipped the formula?

Instead of asking:

- What job do I want?
- How much money do I need?
- What's my title or dream company?

Try asking:

- What do I want my life to *feel* like?
- How much time do I want to spend working?
- How do I want to show up for my family, my health, my peace?
- What role does work play in that vision?

I've been living this second approach for over a decade. In 2007, I sat down and wrote out the vision and values that would guide my business. One thing was clear: I never wanted someone else controlling my time, creativity, or potential. That clarity wasn't just professional—it was personal. I've built a life that allows me to work *with* people, not *for* them. That's alignment.

I've seen friends chase titles that left them empty. I've met lawyers, executives, and entrepreneurs who climbed the ladder only to realize it was leaning against the wrong wall. Because they hadn't checked in with their *why*. They hadn't rooted their vision in their values.

As the band Daughtry once sang:

> "Be careful what you wish for, 'cause you just might get it all—and then some you don't want."

It's time to ask better questions. Not just about what we want to do, but who we want to *be*.

- What kind of life do I want to wake up to each day?
- What pace do I want to move at?
- Who do I want beside me?

This is the heart of conscious lifestyle design, crafting a life from the inside out.

Our values are often inherited, passed down from parents, systems, and culture. But if We don't pause to define our *own*, they will be defined for us.

Right now, ask yourself:

- Am I living in alignment with what matters most to me?
- What have I been tolerating that doesn't match my values?
- What lights me up that I've been ignoring?
- What would I choose if I really believed I had a say?

If these answers bring discomfort, good. Discomfort is the first sign that change is calling. It means we're waking up. And waking up is the first step to reclaiming our lives. We can keep doing what we've always done. Or we can begin designing something that actually fits. Not just a job. Not just a title. A life.

LETTING PASSION GUIDE US

I was at an event networking with other industry professionals when I asked a question to someone I had just met. I asked, "What's your true passion in life? What is the thing you lose yourself in?"

And to dig a bit deeper, I often ask the associated question: "What's your Superpower?"

This woman, who appeared to be in her late thirties, turned to me and said, "I have never in my life had anyone ask me that question before!"

At first, I couldn't tell if she was excited or offended. Then all at once, her eyes lit up, and a big smile ran across her face. She said, "Deep water freediving!"

She went on to tell me of her love of holding her breath and diving to incredible depths, way beyond what I (or most people) would be comfortable doing. My fascination took over. I asked more questions and, simultaneously, watched her body language open up as she waved her hands enthusiastically. She was glimmering with excitement.

The conversation continued. She spoke of her childhood growing up in Saudi Arabia and her love of Heavy Metal music, to which I thought to myself, "Now we are talking!"

Throughout our 15-minute interaction, we didn't talk about work, what we did for a living, or why we were at the conference. We connected as human beings with fascination, curiosity, and presence.

This really is the secret to breaking the ice with another human being. Many people may be shocked and confused when we ask them the question, and in some ways, the magic of the question is not in the question itself, but rather in the intention of the question: "I am interested in who you really are as a person, deeper than the superficialities we tend to default to in conversation."

I have asked this question to others and have turned this question into an exercise for years in my workshops. It always amazes me what profound insight comes out of such a simple little exchange. Some of us love talking about ourselves, while others would rather spend three minutes just listening. Some of us can immediately identify our passions, while others will struggle to come up with something they see themselves as being passionate about. Some will have a hard time stopping their sharing at the three-minute mark, while others will struggle to fill even half of that time with conversation. It's important to ask which we are:

How comfortable am I discussing my passions?

It may be time to redefine the notion of success in life. Most of society measures success by how much money is in our bank account, how nice our house is, and what level of the corporate world we've worked our way up to, but rarely do we measure success based on how connected we are to our passion.

We can start by asking:

What is my true passion in life, the thing I do that I completely lose myself in?

From there, some follow-up questions should be:

- What feelings do I have when I am doing this activity?
- How often do I get a chance to experience my passion?
- Who is with me when I have the experience?
- How much does it cost me to do this?

I have a few passions in life: music, playing guitar, and travel, but when I really think about my daily passion, it looks something like this: I wake up without an alarm, head to the coffee shop, and sit there uninterrupted for as long as I want. It seems so simple, but it's what makes me happy. So, I will run through the questions.

- What feelings do I have when I am doing this activity?
    - Relaxation, enjoyment, freedom

- How often do I get a chance to experience my passion?
    - Daily (or as often as I want)
- Who is with me when I have the experience?
    - Mostly, I'm alone. But it could include being with my sweetheart or working remotely with my brother.
- How much does it cost for me to do this?
    - Somewhere around $3.00

I really can't emphasize or endorse enough how powerful this question has been in my life. So often, we allow all the external pressures to produce, work, and do more, to cloud the things that bring us a sense of fulfillment.

For some, it could be as simple as waking up before the rest of the house or having a designated time to spend with our children. The goal is to assess our relationship with that passion in our current lives.

- How can I focus more of my efforts on doing that thing?
- How much am I willing to change other aspects of my life to fit that in?

Take it a bit deeper and ask:

What is my brilliance in the world?

This asks us to think about what we're best at, or what problem are we great at solving? It could be as nuanced as the feeling we get when we're serving the elderly or writing books like this one. Or, it could be as simple as making people laugh. Whatever it is, ask those questions, and get so super clear on the feeling that comes up when engaging with that thing.

Understanding our passion is a crucial step in life design. However, it's important to recognize that just because our passion is our driving force, it doesn't necessarily have to be our primary source of income. In fact, turning a passion into a job can sometimes diminish the joy it brings. Instead, consider how passion can fit into one's overall lifestyle. Consider:

- What am I really good at?
- What do I do that lights me up?
- How can these skills contribute to a work-life balance that supports my broader life vision?

For example, some might be passionate about writing, but that doesn't mean we have to be a full-time writer. I knew I wanted to write this book, but I never did so with the intention of it making me rich. I've, instead, integrated writing into my life in a way that complements other pursuits and responsibilities.

Ask:

Do I actually have enough time (margin) in my life to enjoy my passions?

The answer is, yes, it just might require shifting some of the focus away from things that do not fuel that passion, even if society tells us we're selfish, or wasting our time, or should be doing something else.

Our most authentic vision is found through our passions and our brilliance (what we are good at), not through societal norms or external pressure. That's the part I want everyone to take away from this, most of all. If we ignore what lights us up, we'll end up chasing someone else's version of success, and it'll never feel satisfying. But when we lean into the things that make us feel most alive, those passions start revealing what we truly value, making the vision clear. And that's the vision that must guide us.

REVEALING THE VISION

Think of life as a series of buckets—each one representing an area that matters to us. For this exercise, we will focus on family, relationships, work, health, and personal growth. Our values and vision should guide how we fill these buckets, helping us stay aligned with what's most important, even when life gets overwhelming.

In the bucket of family, one might include those who matter most to them, considering the role they play in their lives. We can ask:

- What relationships matter most to me?
- How do I want to feel in these relationships?
- What changes could deepen connection or presence?
    - » *I want to feel ________ with ________. I will focus on ________ to strengthen this.*

The work and career bucket often shapes how we spend much of our time, whether it's at the office or at home building our own businesses. We can ask:

- What kind of work energizes me?
- What role do creativity, purpose, or freedom play in my ideal work life?
- What needs to shift in my current work to feel more aligned?
    - » *I thrive when I ________. I'll explore ways to ________ in my current work.*

Now, let's move on to health and well-being, remembering that health isn't just physical—it's mental and emotional, too. This bucket should reflect our ideal state of well-being across all areas. Ask:

- What does thriving feel like in my body and mind?
- What habits support my best self?
- What's one behavior I can begin or return to this week?

» *When I feel ________, I am at my best. I'll commit to ________ to support that.*

If that full picture feels a bit overwhelming, we can try focusing on how we want to feel in our bodies and mind, then let that feeling drive our vision.

We should also have a bucket for our personal growth and fulfillment. This bucket will reflect our ongoing evolution. Think of this part as our "why," the part that brings us closer to our values and the reason we continue to strive, learn, and grow. We can ask:

- What inspires or motivates me?
- What kind of person am I becoming?
- What am I curious to explore or learn more about?

» *My future self is ________. I'll take one small step toward that by ________.*

These questions, inspired by my work receiving certification at Duke University's Integrative Health Coaching program, are designed to help us reflect on how to create a deeper vision for our lives. I recommend writing down the answers to refer back to this sense of clarity on repeat. It's not enough to create a vision once. The process of change requires us to check in, realign, and find ways to stay motivated.

Before we move on to our core values, I want us to pause and reflect on where we are right now, asking ourselves:

- If nothing changes for me, where will I be in 5 to 10 years?
- How does this future compare to the vision I just created?

Remember, this is about identifying small shifts we can make to build momentum toward our ideal future. Each small action brings us closer to what we want, filling our buckets purposefully and intentionally. It's not an opportunity to judge ourselves for the progress we haven't made or the actions we've taken that were counterproductive to our authenticity. Whatever has caused us drama today does not have to be with us in tomorrow's vision. The moment shame, blame, or judgment enters the conversation, it's time to pull out that BS Meter and assess what the false narrative may be.

ALIGNING ACTIONS WITH YOUR VALUES

Imagine values as the foundation beneath each bucket in our lives. These core principles provide meaning and motivation, helping us prioritize the things that matter most—even when life pulls us in conflicting, drama-induced directions. They encompass the behaviors, goals, and ways we consciously choose to live authentically.

First, let's assess the non-negotiable values, the things that we refuse to compromise on. It's essential to identify which values shape our lives and how they influence our behaviors so we can see where small adjustments could bring more alignment between our actions and our values.

This is a list of 50 common core values assembled by author James Clear, which are commonly used by leadership institutes and programs:

Authenticity
Achievement
Adventure
Authority
Autonomy
Balance
Beauty
Boldness
Compassion
Challenge
Citizenship
Community
Competency
Contribution
Creativity
Curiosity
Determination
Fairness
Faith
Fame
Friendships
Fun
Growth
Happiness
Honesty
Humor
Influence
Inner Harmony
Justice
Kindness
Knowledge
Leadership
Learning
Love
Loyalty
Meaningful Work
Openness
Optimism
Peace
Pleasure
Poise
Popularity
Recognition
Religion
Reputation
Respect
Responsibility
Security
Self-Respect
Service
Poise
Popularity
Recognition
Religion
Reputation
Respect
Responsibility
Security
Self-Respect
Service
Spirituality
Stability
Success
Status
Trustworthiness
Wealth
Wisdom

Many experts recommend selecting between five to seven core values to focus on. It may be hard to narrow it down to this number, but we are aiming for the things that take priority.

Looking through the list, it may be helpful to ask:

- What truly matters to me? (Think about values like family, health, work ethic, or spiritual beliefs)
- What are the fundamental beliefs I want to guide my decisions? (Integrity, compassion, family, innovation, etc.)
- Which areas of my life feel most in alignment with my values? Where do I feel most fulfilled?
- Are there areas where my actions go against these non-negotiables? If so, what is preventing change?

Sometimes, our values can feel like they're in conflict, competing with each other for which will win. For example, one's desire for financial security might compete with the value of spending time with family. These moments of conflict can feel like a trap, but they're also an opportunity to clarify what matters most. Recognizing when and where our values conflict empowers us to make intentional decisions and let go of what's less important to prioritize what's essential. Ask:

- Are there two values competing in my life right now?
- If I had to let one go to honor the other, which would I choose?
- What are the top messages or insights I am receiving from this process?

We live in a world of convenience, quick fixes, and immediate results like prescription drugs, A.I., same-day delivery, fad diets, and more. Instant gratification every time, yes. But how do those things reflect our standards, the values that should be guiding our daily actions? Do they move us closer to our vision? Or are they, simply, quick fixes with fading, albeit immediate, results? The latter is not sustainable, that I know for sure.

Living a life that aligns with our vision is not about reaching one-time goals or getting immediate results. It's about creating sustainable habits that reflect our values. Dr. Gabrielle Lyon has talked about how we should shift from outcome-based goals to behavior-driven standards. Instead of "I want to lose 20 pounds" (a goal), it's about shifting to "I exercise daily because it improves my health" (a behavior-driven standard). Focusing on standards moves us away from the cultural obsession with fast results and allows us to begin building habits that last. It keeps us engaged in the process instead of running toward a destination.

But similarly to self-care (which we'll be covering in the next chapter), most of us are constantly getting on and off the train, even when it comes to our values. It's all too easy to focus on the external—what we want to achieve, how far we've come (or not come), or what changes still need to happen.

In this instance, ask yourself:

- What behaviors align with my core values?
- Are there behaviors that don't align with my values? (What might need to change?)
- How do I hold myself accountable to my standards?

Our values ground our vision into reality. Oftentimes, we think of values as abstract principles, but they manifest physically through our actions, decisions, and even our bodies' responses to the world around us. We must tune into our body awareness while reflecting on these values, taking note of how we feel and how our body autonomously reacts to these reflections.

TYING VALUES TO YOUR VISION

Speaking of how the body feels in these instances, let's not forget that when we're out of alignment with our values, our sympathetic nervous system is more prone to running the show. This not only makes it difficult for us to stay grounded, but it causes the vision to become blurry. That's when we end up searching for quick fixes or immediate relief instead of sitting with our value-driven behaviors and decisions rooted in our authentic vision.

This misalignment will cause stress on the body. Remember:

Drama leads to stress which leads to negative outcomes which leads to costs.

Our bodies will manifest anxiety, restlessness, or unease when we're not acting in alignment with our values to bring forth the vision of our lives. After all, we know the ANS is designed to respond to threats, but when we're out of sync with our true selves, it treats those misalignments as a form of threat, triggering stress.

Think of it this way: say our lives are 80% aligned with our values, but there's 20% of things we're doing that we know aren't serving us. Maybe it's a job that goes against our desire for creative freedom or habits that don't honor our health. The body knows this imbalance, even before our mind catches up. The tension builds, and we may feel physically drained, emotionally disconnected, or mentally overwhelmed. This imbalance will impact our ability to fully embrace our vision.

So, how do we bring ourselves back into alignment with our values? The first step is developing body awareness, and paying attention to the signals our body sends when we're stressed or feeling off—tight shoulders, shallow breathing, an upset stomach. These are clues that something in our lives are not aligned with our core beliefs. When we notice these signals, it's time to pause and reflect. We may ask ourselves:

What decision did I make, or what situation am I in, that might be out of sync with my values?

Bridging the mind-body gap means tuning into our body as a compass, helping us course-correct before we drift too far off our authentic path. By regulating our nervous system through practices like deep breathing, meditation, or simply taking a moment to slow down, we can bring ourselves back to a state of safety and calm. This creates the space needed to reassess and realign your actions with our core values.

The more we live in alignment with our values, the more our autonomic nervous system can rest in a regulated state. And when our mind and body are in sync, we can tie our values directly to our vision, creating a life that feels fulfilling and authentic. Even when things diverge from the plan, we'll be better equipped to handle the challenges, knowing that our foundation is built on something true to who we are.

But as I've said, all drama begins and ends with us. To create a fulfilling life vision tied to values that motivate us and represent our authenticity, we've got to:

1. Remind ourselves of our worthiness to create whatever vision for our lives we desire, no matter how big and grand it may seem.
    - *Do I feel worthy of the life I envision for myself?*
    - Remember: We are safe to explore our authenticity.

2. Dismantle the current story we're telling ourselves about why the vision we desire has not come to fruition yet.
    - *What is the story I am telling myself about why this vision is unattainable?*
    - Remember: We can rewire the negative coding your nervous system has grown to believe as the truth.

3. Take accountability for how we have blocked our own vision or lived out of alignment with our values.
    - *What is my contribution to the success and dysfunction in driving my vision forward through my authentic values?*

- Remember: Our role in The Drama Triangle (as the victim, persecutor, or rescuer) is a choice. We can choose neutrality (like the farmer).

4. Assess the aspects of our lives where we feel pressured or uncomfortable taking aligned action. Get clear on the root cause of the conflict and, then, ask how to bring forth a resolution.
    - *What is within my control?*
    - Remember: We are a conscious being experiencing all these inner and outer things, and you are the boss who oversees the mind and body. We do have the ability to lead the team.

5. Get clear on where we're feeding ourselves BS. Consider where we might be deceiving ourselves, or allowing our insecurities to make excuses or justifications that prevent our growth.
    - *What would my life be like in two years if I made this change toward my ideal vision? Or change nothing?*
    - Remember: The drama is the thing that's preventing us from changing.

And when that drama creeps back in—and it will—we may need to yield our sword.

That sword is our tool for cutting through the noise, projection, self-deception, and fear that keep us from seeing the true vision. It helps us tell the truth—to ourselves and to others—about what's best for us. Sometimes, creating a values-aligned life means saying no. No to outdated beliefs. No to other people's expectations. No to anything that dishonors who we really are. The sword helps us make those cuts to liberate us, not from a place of anger, but from unwavering love for the life we're building with intention. That sword guides us to say, "I deserve to feel safe, seen, and in integrity with myself."

But even knowing when to yield that sword takes work. It takes checking in with our EAR—our Empathy, Accountability, and Resilience.

When our values start to drift out of focus, or our vision starts to feel distant, Empathy helps us ask ourselves gently: Where am I overriding what I know to be true?

It allows us to slow down and notice the discomfort without judging it—to sit with the feeling of misalignment and trace it back to its source. Empathy is the doorway to recognition.

Accountability steps in when it's time to realign. It's what asks: Where have I been making choices that contradict the life I say I want? What actions am I taking—or avoiding—that are betraying my values? This is the moment we stop outsourcing responsibility. We take the wheel again, not to punish ourselves, but to redirect with intention.

And then there's Resilience, the part of us that knows how to get back up without abandoning ourselves. It reminds us that vision is a long game. That building a values-led life doesn't happen in one clean motion, it happens through repetition, through returning, through remembering who we are, even when we've temporarily forgotten.

Living in alignment isn't a one-time decision; it's a practice. A daily return. A recalibration of our nervous system, our environment, and our inner beliefs. Over and over again.

So when life shakes your foundation—or when old patterns creep in—pause. Breathe. Ask:

- What truth do I need to see clearly right now?
- What value have I strayed from?
- What would honoring my vision look like today, in this small moment?

Then respond with compassion and kindness. This vision we've unearthed—the one shaped by our core values, the one calling us forward—it's ours. And we are more than capable of protecting it.

Now that we're unearthing your vision and values, the next step is integrating them into how we live, especially how we are investing in our most valuable resource: Ourselves! That's where our next superpower comes forward...

CHAPTER 4:

Activate Your Self-Care - Investing in Inner Wealth

"A fit body, a calm mind, a house full of love. These things cannot be bought- they must be earned."

— Naval Ravikant

Self-care

[self'kâr']

noun

The active process of making your body and mind a pleasant place to inhabit by filling your own cup first. This ensures you have enough to give others. It also ensures you don't burn out and fade away.

I spend a lot of time in elevators.

I know, it sounds weird, but I have come to realize the average elevator ride lasts about 30 seconds, and that is a prime window of opportunity for Eric to practice simple, no-nonsense self-care. I'm being serious here. Here are three self-care practices I have anchored into my psyche to trigger when I get on an empty elevator with no one in it:

- Three physiological sighs

- Ten traditional squats or a yogi squat
- Rapid eye movement exercise

And yes, more than once, the elevator door has suddenly opened with someone's non-verbal communication seemingly saying, "What the hell are you doing in there?"

Another one is when I get in my car. If I can catch myself before I put it in drive, I will stop and take three slow, purposeful breaths before departing.

I invite us to think about what this practice might look like for each of us. Where are those small, open pauses in our day that we can trigger impactful self-care? To begin, this is my main message to you: find small, meaningful ways to take care of our most valuable resource—ourselves!

I've been in the wellness industry most of my adult life. Diet, nutrition, and exercise are important topics that are covered ad nauseam on every major platform. In that spirit, I'm going to sidestep those obvious big buckets and instead focus on some other ideas. For many of us, the big buckets seem daunting and hard to maintain. If there is one theme around self-care that I hear over and over again (as well as experience firsthand), it is this: Self-care is a never-ending process of getting on and off the train. The flow, the struggle, the abandonment, the guilt, the shame, the recovery, the flow...

And once we turn 40, self-care becomes a part-time job—or not.

Perhaps we can agree to start here, then come to a gentle agreement with ourselves around realistic expectations for our wellness. Self-care isn't just about perfecting a downward dog on a sun-soaked beach or sipping green juice while perched on a yoga mat. It's about finding what genuinely recharges you—whether it's a quiet cup of coffee before the house wakes up or a loud karaoke session to '80s hits in your living room.

The irony is not lost on me that while capitalism loves to push products, training, and promises of self-care onto its people, there's also internalized shame associated with making self-care one of your priorities. To combat this, there must be a shift in cultural attitudes recognizing self-care as a fundamental aspect of health and well-being, accessible to all individuals regardless of their socioeconomic status. Though I wouldn't dare say it's our responsibility to change the world's views on self-care, it does begin with us. Promoting a more inclusive and realistic perception of self-care can dismantle the barriers that prevent people from prioritizing themselves.

We don't need to participate in the rat race. That part, like all things, is a choice. After all, we can't pour from an empty cup and certainly can't create a drama-free life when our cup is bone dry.

SELF-CARE = AGENCY OVER COMPORT

Our culture has long struggled with the idea of self-care, at times reducing it to something that feels more trite and superficial than a genuine, necessary practice for well-being. So much of the concept has been externalized to obsess over our physical, or outward, appearance. The discourse revolves around how fit we are and how few wrinkles we have, as if that defines whether or not we're caring for ourselves. The social attitude is built around the ideals of luxury, reserved for those with the time, money, and privilege to indulge in it. It's often equated with pampering or indulgence rather than a necessary holistic practice of nurturing one's physical, emotional, and mental well-being.

At the same time, the expectation is that we must prioritize self-sacrifice, putting others' needs before our own, all while being pressured to hustle and achieve. Each month, we may tend to fill it up with engagements, work, and family. Then, if anything is left over, we come in. Things for oneself often go last. We're conditioned to believe that taking breaks or caring for ourselves is a form of selfishness that's associated with guilt or shame. Self-care is seen as something we do when we don't have "much else" to do or "when we can." There's a pervasive belief that taking time for oneself is synonymous with being selfish or unproductive in other areas, which is simply not true.

Recently, a friend looked at my calendar and exclaimed, "Your Fridays have a lot of white space. Look at that, hardly any meetings! How did you get so lucky?"

I explained that it wasn't a coincidence. This led to a deep conversation about my values and how they dictate my scheduling, especially on Fridays (Drama-Free Fridays, as I like to call them!).

Fridays are the day I intentionally block time to think, wander, go for long slow walks, get a massage, and quite frankly, just be. A jam-packed calendar doesn't mean I'm productive; it just means I'm jumping from call to call, activity to activity, and probably stressed. When I schedule Drama Free Fridays, it's so that I can be more productive, more creative, solve problems easier, and be a kinder human when I am working. And remember, kindness is an Uberpower.

This is step one and possibly the most important step in self-care: staking a claim for the time to invest in ourselves. This is where the path to victory begins.

Just for giggles, try a little experiment with me. Pull up your calendar and take a look at the next full month. Then:

1. Pick a day when you have some margin.
2. Block out a full 2-4 hours and label it as "ME TIME."
3. Choose to do an activity that the deepest part of yourself is longing for: a Tuesday afternoon matinee, an outback hike, or perhaps a 90-minute massage. Write it underneath the "ME TIME" header.
4. Guard the block of time with your life!

I'm serious when I say we should guard the block of time with our lives because they are coming for us: the endless needs of our kids, employers, friends, and family. They will innocently infringe upon the borders of our appointment with ourselves. They mean well, but may ask us to put their needs above ours and inevitably, we will face the decision to protect the sacred time we have gifted ourselves, or we will cave and lose it until the next "ME TIME" which could be next week, next month or maybe 6 months from now.

In my coaching practice, I challenge clients to make two lists:

- List your ideal self-care activities. What would truly feed your body, mind, and spirit?
- Now, list the ones that you actually practice. Is there some discrepancy?

Of course, there may be some discrepancies. So the intent of the exercise is not to feel shame about what we're not doing but rather to run reality through the BS Meter to get clear on the path forward. It's also a time to keep our vision and values at the forefront of our minds. With our vision intact and our values guiding us, these decisions become much easier. We have direction. We know our "why." That'll keep us consistent.

Despite being amidst a wellness movement, there is still some cultural ignorance about self-care in society that most of us participate in, whether consciously or not. Many of us internalize stereotypes rooted in societal expectations and norms, all while silently destroying our self-perception and ability to effectively care for ourselves. For men, self-care and dealing with their emotions in this way has been compared to some lack of masculinity, as if it's a feminine practice men should not need. For women, it seems there's a call to stoicism, to discourage them from prioritizing their needs or risk being seen as vain, indulgent, or self-centered. We are making progress, but there is so much further to go.

Candidly, this is a paradox I encountered in the Health and Wellness industry. The very people educating, inviting, and facilitating self-care for others often weren't very good at taking care of themselves. It is most ironic to me that caregivers struggle to prioritize their self-care in a daily existence of continually providing care to others. This is a perfect example of a misalignment between our comport (our outward behavior) and our agency (our inner capabilities).

The tension between comport and agency is a common reason why self-care is not integrated into many people's daily lives. We are busy doing things that offer us external validation rather than engaging in activities that truly benefit us. Incorporating self-care requires us to shift our focus from external validation (comport) to internal fulfillment (agency). And that's where we get tripped up.

Ask the question:

What is the story I'm telling myself about self-care?

I would bet there's a conflict between comport and agency somewhere in this answer. There's a part of us who knows it's a critical part of being a healthy, functioning human, but there's another part of us who may be focusing on the superficiality of it all.

When I say "the superficiality of it all," I'm talking about how our culture has reduced self-care to something shallow and performative, a checklist of aesthetic achievements rather than a meaningful practice rooted in self-nourishment. We've been conditioned to equate self-care with looking good rather than feeling good, and we prioritize outward appearances over inner peace. The shiny, Instagram-worthy version of self-care—facial masks, spa days, and perfectly curated wellness routines—feels hollow when it's disconnected from what truly sustains us.

This obsession with the surface blinds us to the deeper work of addressing our emotional needs, setting boundaries, and confronting hard truths about our lives. The superficiality serves as a distraction from the real effort required to care for ourselves—an effort that often demands introspection, uncomfortable growth, and a commitment to our own well-being that goes far beyond appearances. True self-care is about honoring our needs in a way that builds resilience and self-trust, not just a temporary fix to cover up the cracks in the foundation.

WHAT HAPPENS WHEN WE STAY OFF THE TRAIN

Neglecting self-care comes at a high price. It impacts the mind, body, spirit, and all of our human experiences. When we forgo self-care, we invite drama and stress into our lives, setting the stage for a multitude of negative outcomes.

Why? Because:

Drama leads to stress which leads to negative outcomes which leads to costs.

When we feel irritable (sometimes all the time), low energy, anxious, withdrawn, tense, etc., it's often because our ANS is dysregulated. That dysregulation is surely going to make us a boat anchor at every party we attend. No one likes a Debby Downer. We know this. It just makes for unnecessary drama. Are we the drama? Probably, if we're feeling all those things, and then trying to authentically engage with the world.

As Thomas Merton wisely observed:

> "To allow oneself to be carried away by a multitude of conflicting concerns, to surrender to too many demands, to commit oneself to too many projects, to want to help everyone in everything, is to succumb to the violence of our times."

Merton wrote these brutally honest words in the 1960s. They hold up well, don't they? The surrender to the relentless demands of modern life can lead to a cascade of stress-related problems, manifesting in our poor mental and physical health.

One of the most profound impacts of neglecting self-care is the toll it takes on our mental health. Dr. Pawlil-Fry highlights the importance of the Brain-Derived Neurotrophic Factor (BDNF), a protein crucial for neuroplasticity. Engaging with stress releases BDNF, which helps rewire our brains to better handle stress, making us more resilient and less likely to spread panic and distress to those around us. However, this beneficial rewiring requires periods of rest and recovery. Without them, BDNF cannot perform its vital role, leaving our brains in constant overdrive. Dr. Pawlil-Fry warns:

> "You need to understand the consequences of not turning off your brain. Of never turning off your phone. Thinking that working longer is the answer. It's not."

Without proper rest, our cognitive functions suffer, and our ability to manage stress effectively diminishes. This may end at the doctor's office in a state of dis-ease.

The American Psychological Association states that as many as 70% of primary care visits are driven by patients' psychological problems, such as anxiety, panic, depression, and stress. There is a slight disconnect here, as a Gallup survey from November 2024 revealed that 75% of U.S. adults desire their primary care providers to address mental health during routine checkups, yet about a third reported never being asked about it. This points to a big responsibility to take agency over our self-care and invest meaningfully.

In the end, what we focus on grows. If we prioritize our well-being, we'll find that our capacity to navigate life's inevitable stresses and challenges increases. We'll be operating from a place of abundance, not scarcity—living in alignment with our values and nurturing the aspects of our life that truly matter.

Physically, lack of self-care can lead to a host of ailments. Chronic stress without adequate recovery can weaken the immune system, increase the risk of cardiovascular diseases, and exacerbate conditions such as hypertension and diabetes. The body requires rest to repair and rejuvenate. We focus more on recharging our iPhones to function properly than on recharging our bodies. Without this downtime, we risk burning out, leading to long-term health complications that are far more challenging to address than they are to prevent.

But no matter how far down the road of illness we might have already traveled, remember that it is always worth it to start the journey back to wellness.

When we are caught up in the whirlwind of constant activity and stress, self-care practices tend to fall by the wayside, leading to a sense of disconnection and imbalance. For those who are spiritually inclined, neglecting self-care can disconnect us from our inner selves and sense of purpose. Spiritual well-being often requires time and reflection, such as meditation, prayer, journaling, or simply being in nature. Research by the EPA (Environmental Protection Agency) suggests that many adults spend less time outdoors than prison inmates due to modern lifestyles, work habits, and increased screen time. The same has been found in American children, as the American Academy of Pediatrics (AAP, 2020) reported that the lack of outdoor play is contributing to rising childhood obesity, anxiety, and attention disorders.

We have to ask ourselves if this spiritual neglect is leaving us feeling hollow, unfulfilled, and potentially contributing as a root cause to many dysfunctions.

OWNING YOUR SELF-CARE JOURNEY

As I've said a time or two now, putting our needs aside is on us. It directly reflects our lack of accountability and autonomy over our lives. It's also a telltale sign that our out-of-whack autonomic nervous system is running the show.

I useful exercise for us is to back to that Drama Triangle and assess if we are playing the victim, the persecutor, or the rescuer regarding self-care.

- Is there a sense of powerless?
- A feeling of incapability with changing the relationship with self-care?
- Or a struggle to assert needs?

Asking this helps us recognize the unconscious roles we might be slipping into—roles that keep us stuck in cycles of burnout, resentment, or avoidance.

If we're the victim, we may tell ourselves there's never enough time, that no one supports us, or that we're too exhausted to prioritize our needs. If we're the persecutor, we might be critical of our attempts at rest, pushing ourselves harder and judging anything less than full productivity. If we're the rescuer, we could be overgiving to others to earn worth or avoid your discomfort, leaving no space for our care in the process.

Identifying the role is the first step. From there, we get to step outside the triangle. We get to choose neutrality, self-responsibility, and conscious care. We get to rewrite the narrative of what self-care means for us, not as a luxury or reward, but as a vital part of living in alignment with our values and vision.

Because the truth is: We can't live a values-aligned life while abandoning ourselves.

Take a moment to reflect on this:

> What is my role in the success or dysfunction of my overall health and well-being?

Don't be surprised if the BS Meter activates heavily during this honest assessment. Ask:

> Where can I hold myself accountable for why self-care remains something I am constantly hopping on and off the train of?

This forces us to think about the thing that usually pushes us off the train and what gets us back on. Whatever's getting us back on is where our authenticity and agency are. Whatever pushes us off, well, that's where we must confront uncomfortable truths about ourselves, requiring deep introspection and honesty.

When we actually commit to self-care, it comes with facing aspects of our lives that we might prefer to ignore, such as unhealthy habits, toxic relationships, or unmet emotional needs. These underlying issues can silently drain our energy and prevent us from fully experiencing the benefits of self-care. To genuinely care for ourselves, we must confront and work through these challenges to make intentional choices that align with our long-term health and happiness. True self-care requires the courage to face discomfort and the discipline to make lasting changes rather than relying on quick fixes that only provide surface-level relief.

One more layer to consider is this: Where we tend to get stuck in the process of change itself. We all move through stages of change (as discussed in Chapter One) when it comes to forming new habits, especially self-care. Maybe we spend a lot of time thinking about what we need (hello, contemplation), but struggle to follow through when it's time to act. Or maybe we go all in for a week and then slide right back into old patterns because there's no structure in place to help us maintain the change. It's not just about willpower—it's about understanding where our resistance lives.

Ask yourself:

- Am I avoiding the first step altogether?
- Am I stuck in planning without execution?
- Am I good at taking action but terrible at consistency?

Knowing which stage tends to trip us up is powerful. It gives us something real to work with instead of spinning in shame or frustration. We can't change what we're unwilling to face, and we can't sustain what we haven't prepared for. Self-care isn't a one-time fix. It's a personal system that must be built stage by stage, with honesty and commitment—all while yielding our Sword of Superpowers at every turn.

This process can be challenging and uncomfortable. It can be difficult to sit with the triggers that keep pushing us off the train. Facing them forces us to confront vulnerabilities and insecurities that we may have been avoiding. Goodness knows we often avoid discomfort at all costs, opting for quick fixes and distractions instead of the work of self-reflection and personal growth. It's often why we stay off the train longer than we're on it. Self-care and self-awareness go hand-in-hand in this instance. They both require us to take a hard look at our behaviors, thoughts, and feelings, acknowledging areas where we may be falling short, such as not setting boundaries, overcommitting ourselves, or neglecting our physical health.

KEEP IT SIMPLE, DUDE

In a culture that often glorifies constant productivity and achievement, it can be uncomfortable for me to admit when we need rest or that today, nothing is getting done on the "top priority" list. We don't often allow ourselves permission to take breaks, say no to additional responsibilities, and prioritize our own needs without feeling guilty. Without a level of discipline and resilience, most people are too exhausted or scared to commit to this work.

Resilience, adaptability, and discipline are essential when it comes to self-care because they enable us to navigate the complexities and challenges of life's drama while maintaining our well-being. It is necessary to look deeply into our inner truths and understand what we truly want and need. This introspection helps identify the underlying motivations and barriers to self-care. But then we've got to set all the BS aside, put blinders on, and work resiliently toward those wants and needs.

We need to balance our external comport with our internal agency, all while taking action that fully aligns with those inner desires and not our external expectations. And that's precisely where most of us fall short. We're programmed to be corporate robots, not autonomous human beings. We're often running on autopilot. To combat this tendency to run on autopilot, the next self-care strategy has worked well for me. And as I often say to myself: "Keep it simple, dude."

Take out your phone for a minute and open up a blank doc in an app like "Notes" or "Pages." We are going to establish a list of five things we can do right now, in this moment, that will invest in your self-care. Here is what my list (in no particular order) currently looks like:

1. Send a text of appreciation to someone I love
2. Drink a big glass of water
3. Eat a spoonful of fermented food (kimchi is my jam!)
4. Do three physiological sighs (there it is again!)
5. Get eight hours of rest

What is on your list? It might surprise some of us how simple it could be. Maybe it's finally scheduling that long-overdue doctor's appointment, stepping outside for ten minutes of fresh air, or deleting the app that steals your energy.

The point is: these choices are ours. They don't need to be immeasurable. They just need to be intentional. Real self-care is about becoming someone who shows up for their vision, their values, and their well-being... again and again.

And when it feels hard to do that—when the guilt creeps in, when the world feels too noisy, or when you're caught between what we need and what we've been conditioned to prioritize—that's when we reach for our sword. Not to fight, but to cut through the distractions, the perfectionism, the shame, and the performance. To slice away anything that doesn't serve our journey.

The sword reminds us that every time we make a simple, intentional choice that honors our needs, we are taking powerful, aligned action. No drama. No justification. Just truth and care. Keep it simple, and when in doubt, lead with the sword.

MAKING INVESTMENTS IN THE BUSINESS OF US

Self-care is fundamentally an inside job. While we cannot change the external world, we can transform our interpretation and involvement with it through the work we do on ourselves. This transformation requires a healthy mind, body, and spirit. Without this inner harmony, our efforts to manifest our desires are futile.

Think of self-care as part of the user manual for being human. Skipping the maintenance section might save time in the short run, but eventually, something's going to break down. It's like trying to run a marathon without ever taking a break or refueling—sooner or later, we're going to hit a wall.

This is where the concept of compound interest comes into play. You've probably heard ad nauseam about the power of financial prowess as it relates to the magic of compound interest—the idea that small, consistent investments grow exponentially over time. But this principle doesn't just apply to money; it applies to self-care, too.

Envision our autonomic nervous system (ANS) as a bank account. We make deposits consistently so that when we need to withdraw—when stress hits, when we're triggered, when life throws chaos our way—we have enough reserves to keep us steady. Many people are tuned in to their financial flow all month long, tracking what goes in and what comes out, ensuring they don't overdraft. They understand that saving and investing consistently creates long-term stability.

Our ANS operates the same way. When we make regular self-care investments—whether through rest, movement, boundaries, or mindfulness—we aren't just maintaining balance; we're building resilience that compounds over time. Each small act of regulation strengthens our system, creating a foundation that allows us to handle stress more effectively in the future. Just like financial investments grow through compounding, the more we tend to our nervous system, the more capacity we build to navigate life without depleting ourselves.

By recognizing what triggers, drains, and disrupts our flow, we can be intentional about making deposits that serve us in the long run. If we wait until we're in the red to start caring for ourselves, we're constantly playing catch-up. But when we invest consistently, we create a surplus—a buffer that ensures we don't just survive stressful moments but move through them with greater ease.

For example, I regularly invest in the following, which align with my vision and values:

1. My mental, emotional, physical, and spiritual well-being
2. My partner/marriage
3. My family and siblings
4. My friends
5. My bank and financial accounts
6. My continued education and professional development

In contrast, here are some areas of life I no longer invest in:

1. Giving unsolicited advice
2. Needing to prove I'm right
3. Understanding the reasons behind the "drama" behavior of others
4. Changing anyone
5. Letting people talk endlessly about themselves in social situations (ie, "Please excuse me, I have to run to the restroom!")
6. Being out past 10:00 pm
7. Giving away professional coaching time

Warren Buffett once said:

"The difference between successful people and really successful people is that really successful people say 'no' to almost everything."

Time is a precious, finite resource. From an investment standpoint, to get the highest return, we have to be able to say "no" to people and opportunities that don't directly benefit our personal or professional interests. Like any investment, there is a balance statement. This is concretely practiced through deposits, withdrawals, and overdrafts.

Every time we engage in activities or habits that support our well-being, we're making deposits. This could be something as simple as taking a walk, spending quality time with loved ones, or deciding to say no to that engagement. These actions strengthen our ability to cope with future stressors, just like adding money to a savings account builds our financial safety net.

On the flip side, every time we neglect self-care, push ourselves too hard, or ignore our own needs, we're making withdrawals from our account. These withdrawals are sometimes necessary, just as financial withdrawals are part of managing any account. But over time, if we keep making withdrawals without replenishing our resources, we risk depleting our reserves entirely, leading to burnout, illness, or emotional exhaustion. Overdrafts, the constant draining of energy without sufficient deposits, can leave us feeling bankrupt, unable to manage even the smallest stressor effectively.

The key is finding a balance: knowing when to say no, as Warren Buffett suggests, and being mindful of where we're investing our time, energy, and emotional resources.

Consider this:

- Am I building compound interest in the areas of life that matter most to me?
- Am I taking proactive steps to ensure that my physical and emotional 'bank account' is healthy?

These are the questions we need to ask ourselves regularly to maintain that balance. One of the most important being:

Am I worthy of investing in myself?

Some of us will probably say yes and then quickly ramble off the list of reasons why it's just not that easy. "Yes, Eric, I'm worth the investment, but I just don't have it to give." Well, why not? Ask:

- What else is going on that's draining my resources and energy?
- What else am I investing in that is preventing me properly caring for myself?

Like I said, this is a personal bank account. If there's an overdraft, it's on us to sit with our finances and realign our budget. Mur mind, bodies, and soul should be no different.

We are worth that investment, even if it means taking some super challenging steps to make that investment—even if it pisses people off. So, knowing we are worthy of the investment, it's time to start depositing—and that's non-negotiable.

NAVIGATING YOUR PATH TO SELF-CARE

Just as small, regular contributions to a savings account grow over time, so do self-care habits. Each small act of self-care accumulates, building momentum and yielding long-term benefits. This extends to all areas of life—relationships, finances, and personal well-being. By consistently investing in ourselves, we not only experience immediate benefits but also establish a foundation for ever-evolving growth and contentment.

There is no one way to do this. Let me say that. There is no one way. In fact, some methods are not feasible for all people. Uncovering what we need to feel good is nonlinear. That's why owning our self-care journey involves deep introspection.

Ask yourself:

What is in my control when it comes to self-care?

This is an important question because it shifts our focus from what we can't control—external events, other people's expectations, the chaos of daily life—to what we can. It invites us to take ownership of our well-being, acknowledging that self-care is an intentional process. Too often, we default to reacting to life rather than proactively shaping it. We hand over control to circumstances, letting them dictate how we feel, how we show up, and how we care for ourselves. By asking this question, we reclaim our power. We realize that while we can't control everything, we can choose how we care for ourselves in the face of unpredictability.

This question lays the groundwork for creating a drama-free life. Drama often stems from unmet expectations, external pressures, or the feeling that life is happening *to* us rather than *for* us. When we focus on what is within our control, we begin to eliminate unnecessary chaos. We reduce our reliance on external validation and free ourselves from the pressures of comparison. Our choices—whether to engage in drama or choose peace, whether to hold onto resentment or practice forgiveness—become clearer when we are in tune with our internal needs. This is why self-care, at its core, is about perspective. It's about how we engage with ourselves, our bodies, and the world around us.

Early in my career as a massage therapist, I worked with a young woman in her mid-thirties. She came into my office complaining of neck and shoulder pain, then, with great intensity, declared, "I am never, never, ever getting married again!" She waved her finger at me, her anger palpable and surprising.

As she vented, I shifted my attention to her body—her musculature, bone structure, and posture. What I saw was a torso seemingly armored, with her back and shoulders rounding as though bearing the weight of the world. It was as if her heart had sunk into the quicksand of her ribcage. Her entire being screamed of fight, flight, or freeze, with one clear mission: protect herself.

I quickly realized her anger wasn't directed at me but at the world. She was in survival mode, shielding herself from everything and everyone. This woman may have come to me for a therapeutic massage (which is absolutely a form of self-care), but her body told me the type of self-care she needed required much more than a massage. This woman needed to heal inner wounds that a massage could help begin the process of letting go, but she was not going to get to the root of her issue. She needed to feel safe, to trust the world again. The type of investments she needed to make in her ANS bank account to get to that place would not have been solved solely through a massage.

There's substantial evidence showing that massage therapy can downregulate the autonomic nervous system (ANS), lower cortisol levels, and reduce stress-related hormones while boosting serotonin and dopamine. These biochemical shifts promote relaxation and emotional release, often allowing the body to move out of a chronic stress state and into rest and recovery. This is one of the reasons I regularly invest in receiving massage and bodywork. Massage has been very, very good to me.

But here's the thing: while massage or any complementary health approach can help facilitate internal changes, it's only part of the equation for deep, lasting healing. In the case of this woman, her physical tension was rooted in emotional trauma and unresolved pain. No amount of massage could untangle the deep-seated patterns of fear, distrust, and anger that had taken hold of her body and mind. The real work for her required emotional and psychological healing, which involves processing past experiences, rebuilding a sense of safety, and learning how to trust again. Massage can create the space for that healing to begin, but true self-care in her case went far beyond the surface-level benefits of physical touch—it required a deep investment in her inner emotional landscape.

We can facilitate that healing through other forms of body-centered work, too. It's known as somatic healing. As opposed to cognitive healing, which focuses on changing dysfunctional thought patterns and beliefs to improve our well-being, somatic healing focuses on emotional issues through the body-mind connection and bodily experiences. It assists the ANS in transitioning from arousal to relaxation. Through heightened body awareness, we can detect early signs of ANS dysregulation, like increased heart rate or shallow breathing. By honing in on bodily sensations, movements, and tension patterns, we are aiding our ability to connect with the body through our minds so the two can work together. That is the essence of self-care.

There are countless attainable, tangible ways to get connected to the self without feeling like we have to surrender to a vow of silence at an ashram or go on an all-encompassing journey to find ourselves (unless that's what we want to do). Like the practice of jumping. Hear me out!

Jump movement is a powerful, accessible form of somatic healing that can provide immediate benefits to our ANS. It involves short bursts of controlled, rhythmic jumping, sometimes for as little as 2-5 minutes per session. This movement stimulates the lymphatic system, which is crucial for boosting immune function while also releasing endorphins, the body's natural mood elevators. By engaging in jump movement, we help release stored tension, recalibrate our nervous system, and bring the body into a more balanced, relaxed state. It's a form of self-care that's easy to incorporate into daily life, requiring no special equipment or setting. The act of jumping connects us to the body in a way that's both playful and energizing, reminding us that healing can be dynamic and doesn't always have to be solemn or still.

But it is not necessarily the methods that I want readers to take away from this book. Remember, this is not a one-way process that works for everyone. I want us to work toward inherently following the cyclic path of growth, adaptation, and renewal inside us, even when we aren't consciously recognizing it. My goal is for people to craft a plan and engage in it with the conscious intention of establishing a strong foundation for clarifying their authentic desires and creating the life they truly want, regardless of their life phase.

In my decades as a wellness practitioner, educator, and consultant, I've witnessed many things science can explain—and many it cannot. In the healing arts, there is a balance between evidence-based practice and practice-based evidence. I believe this principle is key to creating a drama-free life. Too much reliance on concrete evidence can disconnect us from the mysteries of life, while too much "woo-woo" leaves us vulnerable to ungrounded, sham approaches. Finding a balance between the two—combining allopathic medicine with healing arts like massage and Reiki—enables a more holistic path to wellness.

What I want readers to take away is the understanding that true self-care is about finding what works for us as individuals, beyond the methods prescribed by others. It's about learning to listen to your inner rhythms and allowing space for growth and renewal without getting lost in rigid frameworks or fleeting trends. The journey toward authentic well-being requires that we tune into both the practical and the intuitive aspects of your health—what science can measure and what only your body, mind, and spirit can feel. It's not about picking one method or another but about blending them in a way that honors your unique needs. Healing is not linear or one-size-fits-all; it's deeply personal, and the path to wholeness is one only we can map out for ourselves.

FROM ROOTS TO GROWTH

Humans, unlike most mammals, walk through life on two legs, exposing our most vulnerable part—our soft underbelly—directly to the world. This area receives both the kindness and love sent our way, as well as the arrows of pain and suffering. In the Ayurvedic system, this vulnerability is represented through the chakras—spinning wheels of energy that connect our physical and emotional well-being. This duality of openness and protection is a reminder of how we engage with life's challenges and opportunities.

This constant exposure of our underbelly—both physically and metaphorically—reflects the delicate balance we must strike between vulnerability and self-preservation. In the context of self-care, this is highly relevant because it reminds us that true self-care is not about building walls to shield ourselves from pain (like the client I mentioned) but rather about creating a space where we can experience both love and hardship without losing our sense of self. The Ayurvedic concept of the chakras highlights the connection between our physical bodies and emotional experiences, urging us to nurture not only our outer defenses but also our inner energy systems. When we neglect this deeper level of care, we risk closing ourselves off, living in survival mode, and missing out on life's opportunities for growth and connection. Self-care, then, becomes not just about pampering the body but about healing and balancing the energy that flows within us so that we can face the world with strength and openness.

To share my experiences and insights as a recovering drama magnet who has used this work to design a life of contentment, I want us all to prioritize internal exploration over external validation, authenticity, and truth over status quo and BS. All while using the ANS to guide us. And if the ANS is going to guide us, we need to actively care for and nurture it.

That's why, to be the regulator of our nervous systems, we first need to feel safe in our bodies. That's what enables us to make decisions that best serve us. It's the lack of self-trust that causes a dysregulated system because we have no landing place that feels good. It all becomes misguided energy. And that is one sure way to fight the river. But remember, we don't want to fight it; we want to feel safe riding the waves. Feeling safe riding the waves means we are attuned to what our body needs to stay afloat. And we must honor that intuition by following through and giving our bodies what they need.

When life gets loud, resistance creeps in, or we're tempted to abandon our self-care entirely, we can use EAR to stay present with ourselves through the discomfort of growth.

- Empathy reminds us to start with curiosity, not criticism. When our system is signaling burnout, depletion, or avoidance, empathy helps us ask, *"What's underneath this?"* instead of spiraling into guilt or shame.

- Accountability brings us back to our choices. It helps us name where we've drifted from our values or vision and ask, *"What do I need to shift so I can show up differently?"*

- Resilience is what keeps us grounded when progress isn't linear. It reminds us that returning to our practices—over

> and over again—is still growth. That we don't have to be perfect, just present.

EAR helps us tune into our body's signals without bypassing them or bulldozing through them. It anchors us in the kind of self-honesty that fuels change, not sabotage. It's our built-in check-in system to support nervous system regulation, energy alignment, and decision-making rooted in who we actually are, not who we think we have to be.

In many ways, self-care is the bridge between survival and thriving. But what does it really mean to care for ourselves? To rewrite the narrative that self-care is indulgent, we must first understand it as essential and non-negotiable. When we approach self-care as a foundation rather than an escape, we create a life where resilience and peace coexist. It's no longer about pampering ourselves to temporarily escape drama; it's about cultivating clarity and balance so that drama loses its grip on us entirely.

Understanding the ANS is a crucial part of this journey. The ANS is like the river that runs through the roots of our being, regulating everything from how we react to stress to how we connect with joy. When we are dysregulated—when fear, mistrust, or societal pressure hijack this system—we lose our sense of safety and self-trust. But when we prioritize self-care, we become the regulator. We attune to our body's signals, listen to its wisdom, and respond with compassion and action.

Self-care allows us to feel safe riding the waves of life, no matter how turbulent. It's not about avoiding the river's flow but about learning to float, to trust, and to steer with intention. When we create this foundation, we stop fighting the current and start navigating with grace.

So, the question that remains to be asked is:

> Am I ready to plant my roots and grow into the fullest version of myself?

Now's the time to assess who the "fullest version of ourselves" is and what truly matters to us. It's our chance to unearth the vision and values for the life we so desire, with intention, authenticity, and wellness at the forefront.

CHAPTER 5:

Activate Your Life Design – Designing From the Inside Out

"Set peace of mind as your highest goal, and organize your life around it."

— Brian Tracy

At 13, I tried out for the junior varsity basketball team. I was all about sports until that point, but then my passion shifted to the guitar. I found myself playing my guitar far more than practicing basketball. Despite my dad and peers insisting I stay with sports because I had a lot of future potential, I realized that my heart wasn't in it. The turning point came when I failed to condition myself physically for the upcoming basketball season, particularly with the amount of running we were asked to do in the first practice. After only 20 minutes of running drills, I ran to the bathroom and got violently ill. My body let me know it was time to quit and follow my own path. At that moment, my vision shifted from sports to music, and I had to listen to that inner voice, despite external pressures to stay with sports. And I never looked back or regretted my decision.

In a similar vein, I found myself internally conflicted during my first semester of college. Should I stay or should I go? After only a couple of months, I found myself miserable and concluded that my heart wasn't in it. Coming home for Thanksgiving break, I was surprised when many of my peers voiced similar sentiments about their first semester. They, too, were unsure about the college path and the school they had chosen. When I mentioned that I might quit because I was unhappy, the majority of them thought I was nuts and that I should stick it out. "You can't quit! I'm miserable too, but I'm not going to disappoint my parents, and you shouldn't either."

I started listening to my body, and my stomach was in knots thinking about going back after the holiday. My anxiety was peaking. The voice in my head kept asking, "Why would I stay where I'm not happy?" So, I bravely declared at the end of the first semester that I would not return for the second. I quit and decided to pursue a music career. Eventually, I did return to a different college and thrived.

These moments taught me to trust the signals from within, whether it was my gut, my energy, or my anxiety. That internal feedback became the compass I've followed ever since.

Had I listened to external voices and opinions about my life choices, I might never have gotten good at playing the guitar. I also might have spent another three and a half years being really unhappy at college. In both instances, the essence of the question I was asking myself was:

Where does my agency lie in this situation I'm encountering?

That question is a catalyst. It is the one that allowed me to activate the agency I always knew I had to design a life that fit my passions. The activation process may not have been smooth sailing at times. It still isn't in certain moments of my life (like trying to write this book), but I vowed not to allow anyone else to design my life but me. And I meant it. That, in many ways, is the essence of creating a drama-free life.

WHAT IS LIFE DESIGN?

Life design involves thoughtfully crafting our daily lives, environments, relationships, and careers to match our internal compass. The process transforms abstract concepts of what we envision for our lives into actionable steps, ensuring that our lifestyle supports and reflects our deepest aspirations. Leaving basketball to pursue music and quitting college to pursue a music career are examples of how I drowned out all the noise and listened to my body—my internal compass—and it always served me well to do so.

We could say this entire book is built on designing our ideal life. All roads can lead to contentment, and the path to contentment is paved by how we design our lives. My journey taught me the importance of listening to my inner voice. Even as a young boy, going against the wishes of my Dad (who was my only hero) and telling him I didn't want to play sports anymore was a significant moment. My Dad didn't fully understand, and my jock friends shunned me for quitting, but that decision was crucial. Transitioning from an athlete to a musician allowed me to travel more, make more money, have more fun, and meet more people throughout the span of my life. I still play the guitar, a passion that has enriched me personally far more than basketball ever could.

Life design is all about knowing what we want and living through it. It's about creating a sustainable, ideal existence where every external element—from our jobs to our relationships—forms a solid foundation for a fulfilling life. When our external world reflects our internal values, we achieve a deep sense of contentment that transcends external circumstances. By listening to my inner voice and pursuing what truly resonated with me, I built a life based on my values first, not a system's or another person's.

The essence of life design is knowing what we want, having the courage to pursue it, and creating a life that excites us, no matter how much we might fear what others might think.

As Bernard Baruch said:

> "Be who you are and say what you feel because those who mind don't matter and those who matter don't mind."

DESIGNING WITH THE NERVOUS SYSTEM IN MIND

As with all concepts addressed in this book, none of this is black and white. We understand to this point that the regulation of our autonomic nervous system is not a quick fix or something that can be forced. It is a process, one that requires patience, reflection, and a deep dive into how our internal system is working with us (or against us). Much of that is dependent on how safe we feel in our bodies, in our environments, and how much we trust the people we interact with and share life with. This is a highly personal, deeply introspective journey that likely brings up trauma, unprocessed emotions, and difficult memories—things many of us have pushed aside for too long. But through the visions and values we set for our lives (the ones that cannot be based on the expectations or judgments of others), we feel a sense of direction while we embark on that journey.

That's why destigmatizing self-care and seeing it as a self-investment is key. Without self-care, we can't effectively manage our energy, our boundaries, or our emotional responses. But it doesn't look the same for everyone. How each of us cares for ourselves is unique to us, and the time it takes to form new habits around that care may be different for each of us.

This one life, above all, is for us and us alone. And how close we'll get to that most authentic version of ourselves, how we'll figure out the steps to actively design our lives, well, that part's up to us—and that's a powerful thing. True life design begins by asking the question:

> How willing am I to embrace this change, to confront discomfort, and release patterns that no longer serve me?

I never said it'd be easy, but I did say it'd be worth it. I stand on that.

CHANGE IS THE INEVITABLE PATH TO GROWTH

For the longest time, I would exclaim, "I want to live in a hotel."

Friends would think I was saying it in jest, but for me, it was part of my vision for the future. Simple, elegant living with minimal possessions.

At the beginning of the 2020 pandemic, I was living alone and realized very quickly that my mental health was deteriorating with each passing day. Devoid of the life I knew as an extrovert, where I travelled often and was around people daily, I realized my isolation was not going to be sustainable. I packed up my apartment and moved in with friends for four months. The next two years would find me staying with friends and family and living the life of a digital nomad with no proper home address. It was a necessary step for me as the pandemic went on for much longer than most of us thought. As society began to open up again, I found myself living in hotels, Airbnbs, B&Bs, as well as within the company of friends and family. Honestly, it felt adventurous, fun, and was a relatively stress-free existence.

After three years of living nomadically, the external voices grew louder. Well-meaning family and friends insisted I needed a "real home" to be grounded. I gave it a try, but my body quickly reminded me I'd veered off path.

Over the 12 months of my lease, I spent very little time in my apartment, and when I was there, I felt isolated, like I had made a mistake. I caved to the external pressure and expectations of those who were really well-meaning, but had no idea what was right for me or how I wanted to move through my life.

So I sat down with the Rhythm of Change in front of me and asked myself, "What needs to change for me right now, and what does the next phase of my life look like?"

Once again, I decided the vision for my life was to live in a hotel, and off I went into the life I knew without a home. Five of the last six years, I have lived off the grid of a traditional lifestyle. When people ask where I live, I would say, "Chapel Hill, North Carolina," but in reality, I lived day to day and week to week wherever my work and my desire found me. When I would feel vulnerable enough to share this fact with someone, many times I was met with the projection they would put on me. Things like:

- "Ugh, I feel so sorry for you having to live in a hotel."
- "It must be so stressful having to move all of the time."
- "You never get to sleep in your own bed, that sounds like hell."
- "How can you have any pets if you're always traveling?"
- "What are you running from?"

Realizing these questions weren't worth answering, I would often default to telling people I lived in North Carolina and let sleeping dogs lie. Then I realized it was a lie. I live wherever I want, and it is okay for me to own that truth without worrying about what other people say, think, or feel. This, my friends, is the essence of life design.

And yes, claiming life on our own terms is often very difficult not only to structure but to declare and own in the face of others' projections and judgments. Nevertheless, it's the path we may decide to take. In fact, I am inviting us all to take this journey for ourselves here and now. This chapter is all about offering guidance through the process of designing life on our own terms, grounded in our vision and values.

It's worth noting that some of us have more external commitments than others; family, children, pets, mortgages, brick and mortar businesses, etc., that require us to consider those very important aspects of our lives as we design our future. Whether we have all of the aforementioned commitments or are a solo act, we have an incredible amount of personal agency to design the life we want.

Taking authentic, actionable steps to design our ideal reality depends on our readiness for change and how prepared we are for things to go sideways at any moment. That's why many of us stay in these seemingly comfortable lives even though we're taking actions and making decisions that are not at all aligned with our passions or authenticity. We're not ready to look change in the face, nor are we prepared to handle the challenges that come our way when we step outside of that comfort zone to embrace change instead of resisting it.

Fundamentally, life is full of suffering and unavoidable change. Acknowledging this truth allows us to navigate it, embrace pain as a teacher, and trust that working through it will lead to a better place. That's the truth of resilience. We've got to find a way to not get too high, or sit too low, but find a place right in the middle where we can seek safety amidst the discomfort and pain that comes with changing.

But our life's vision needs us to be active participants, not just daydreamers. Daydreaming matters. Please do not misconstrue. It's just not the full picture. To get clear on what we want and then act on it requires us to get uncomfortable. We have to believe it can be our truth. We have to believe we can, and will, change for that vision. That's where it starts to get sticky for us.

If we were sitting together right now and I asked: "Where does the path lead?" What would the answer be?

Let's say the answer is that the path for leads to a quaint cottage by the sea, with a room overlooking the water to paint and make pottery, and watch the sunrise from the bedroom balcony. On that path, you're hosting workshops for aspiring clay artists and conducting yoga classes at your friend's studio on Wednesday nights. You've met a partner who respects and honors you. You feel confident when you walk into a room. You go to bed at night knowing no one can penetrate your contentment but you.

That all sounds beautiful, doesn't it? That's a desirable vision. Many of us could get lost in that vision. Some might even be reading this, saying, "Wow, Eric! That's the exact life I envision for myself!"

But now, let's say I ask the question, "What's stopping you?" There'd most likely be a freeze point, a visceral sensation in the stomach, blood possibly racing a bit more than it was during that whole visualization of life by the ocean. You might be starting to think about the current, unhealthy relationship you're in (but want out of), the family members who might think your choices are all too out of reach, the money you don't have to buy said quaint cottage, all the people, places, and things that could, maybe, possibly, potentially prevent you from growing into that version of yourself. It all starts to sound and feel pretty uncomfortable once we let all those thoughts get to us, doesn't it? We start to believe it can't possibly be true, not with all those hurdles to climb! We often convince ourselves that we cannot change. But I'm here to invite you to the possibilities!

The wiring of our brains and the experience of change are deeply intertwined. We already know we're hellbent on survival. This prioritization of survival has led us to three fundamental drives: control, stability, and avoidance of pain. However, these drives are not always reflective of reality. We are interconnected with our environment and subject to constant change.

Our brains form neural pathways based on habitual behaviors that become comfortable to us over time. Comfort often arises from these well-worn pathways, leading to a reluctance to deviate. As a result, we become satisfied with the status quo, resisting change that might be beneficial.

To illustrate this point, let's try a simple somatic exercise together.

Fold your arms without thinking about it. Then, look at which arm is resting on top of the other. (For me, my right arm sits on top of my left.) Now, slowly break your arms apart and refold your arms with the other arm on top. Do this slowly so you can feel the synapses in your brain process the new neural pathway. Does it feel a bit unfamiliar?

You can do the same type of exercise by intertwining your fingers together in a clasped hand position. Then, look at what thumb is sitting on top of the other. Now, slowly break your hands apart and interlace your fingers together with the other thumb on top, and notice what happens in your nervous system. For the majority of us, the new pathway may feel awkward, unfamiliar, or strange. The change in our habitual pattern moves from unconscious to conscious repatterning of a "new way of doing things."

To navigate change effectively, we must understand the role of discomfort and uncertainty in helping us get to the next phase. Creating a vision serves as a motivator for embracing that discomfort. It sets the stage for behavior change and establishes motivation rooted in personal values. As the main character of our vision, it's our job to consciously interact with the mind and body to fulfill those aspirations.

This is why it's so important to pause here and ask yourself again:

Where does the path lead for me? And just as importantly: What's stopping me from walking it?

It's an invitation to get real about how change actually happens. If you've been following along, you already know that change isn't a straight line; it's a cycle, a rhythm. And it's messy. So let's name it.

- Which stage of change am I in right now when it comes to my vision?
- Am I still circling in that *awakening* phase, imagining a new life but not yet ready to take action?

Some of us may be deep in the *expansion* phase, testing new boundaries, only to feel overwhelmed by all the unknowns. Perhaps some of us feel *stability* but are struggling to keep it going, or are in a *closure* season, needing to let go of something old before we can fully step into the new.

No stage is better than another. But knowing where we get stuck most often is crucial. It's like taking an ANS check-in. We can ask ourself things like things like:

- Is my body responding with *fight*—pushing too hard, overcommitting?
- With *flight*—avoiding, procrastinating, numbing out?
- Or with *freeze*—feeling hopeless, paralyzed, unable to take a step forward?

Remember what we've learned about Polyvagal Theory. When we feel safe and regulated in our bodies, our ventral vagal system is online, supporting connection, creativity, and clear thinking. When we're stressed or overwhelmed, our sympathetic system may kick in, pushing us into overdrive. And when we feel defeated or trapped, we might drop into dorsal shutdown, disconnected and depleted.

This is why self-awareness is so important. Knowing where we are in the stages of change—and how our nervous system is responding—gives us the tools to move through it. We can catch the signs when we're slipping into old patterns or getting stuck in a cycle of resistance. And then, we can bring in our support systems:

- Self-awareness from our body's cues
- Compassion for the stage we're in
- Courage to take the next step

Think of it this way: we already have the tools. We've learned how to invest in our self-care, how to define our vision, how to name our values, and how to build safety and trust in our bodies. We've learned how to recognize when we're playing the victim, the persecutor, or the rescuer. And we've got the Sword of Superpowers in our back pocket as a reminder that we can cut through the noise, the fear, the old stories, and the external expectations.

Sometimes, we'll need to draw the sword, say no, set a boundary, and make a bold move that aligns with our truth. Other times, the sword stays sheathed, and we pause to listen, reflect, and recalibrate. Either way, our job is to stay connected to our EAR. Our empathy will help us soften toward our stuck places without self-blame. Accountability will help us own our choices and actions. Resilience will keep us moving, even when it's messy. This is how we stop fighting the river and start designing a life that reflects our deepest truth.

Somatic practices are great for this type of work because they're all about integrating the body, mind, and spirit to create wholeness.

Somatics integrates the physical, emotional, mental, and spiritual dimensions of being. Bodywork, yoga, tai chi, dance, meditation, creative arts, and more are all modalities of somatic practices meant to help us process and release stored trauma, restoring a sense of safety, resilience, and empowerment within us.

I think of the Yogi Squat, in this instance. This is a deep squatting position where the feet are flat on the ground, the knees are bent, and the torso is lowered between the thighs with hands pressed together in a prayer position. Originating from ancient Indian yoga practices, this pose helps open the hips, stretch the lower back, and improve ankle mobility. It also aids in digestion, stimulates the pelvic floor, and encourages a calming, grounding effect on the body, making it beneficial for both physical flexibility and mental relaxation. To regulate the body, holding this pose for 30 seconds to 2 minutes, while focusing on deep, steady breaths, can be effective.

Practices like this require us to get uncomfortable while we adjust to the transformations that occur, but it beats making choices that are off-value to our authenticity. That has even more repercussions. Richard Strozzi-Heckler says:

> "When we no longer are afraid of who we are, we act from integrity and authenticity."
>
> Ask yourself:
>
> If I step outside of fear and act solely from my authenticity, how different would the action steps toward my vision be? How much more willing might I be to move through the rhythm of change in my life?

We both know it'd be a helluva lot easier for us all if we didn't have an external standard we thought we had to follow (even though we don't). If we could play by our own rules. And that's the thing, really. Life design does require us to play a game, and we're the one who chooses which game we play.

WHAT GAME ARE YOU PLAYING? CHOOSING YOUR PLAYER

When we were children, we were often asked, "What do you want to be when you grow up?" This question, while well-intentioned, sets a limiting framework for our future aspirations. It nudges us toward identifying with a specific role or profession rather than considering the broader picture of what we want our lives to look like. As we grow, we become so focused on achieving that "thing" that our identity becomes intertwined with it (or lost in it), often at the expense of other important aspects of our lives. We end up playing a game we didn't actually choose to play, not from a place of our authentic vision and values.

Naval Ravikant, an entrepreneur and thought leader, developed a concept of life as a series of games. It offers a valuable perspective for life design in this instance. Society wants us to buy into this idea that we're all playing a multi-player game. One where we hustle for other people, for social validation, for measures of success defined by other systems or organizations. It's this one-size-fits-all, multi-player game, where everyone is chasing the same rewards of wealth, status, and external approval. One where we're all enslaved to one particular meaning for how our lives should be designed. Ask yourself:

> "What is the story I am telling myself about how I should design my life?"

To go deeper, ask where this story came from and what systems, people, or parts of society led you to believe it as your truth.

Ravikant's perspective offers validation that we create our own meaning and our own interpretation of what our lives look like. We are the creators and the makers of our destiny. Playing a multiplayer game strips us of our agency. It makes us feel like we're not in control. It's competitive and external and driven by the pressure to "be something" when we grow up, rather than just being and having that be enough.

Ravikant challenges us to reject the notion of these multiplayer games. He says:

> "The reality is life is a single-player game. You're born alone. You're going to die alone. All of your interpretations are alone. All your memories are alone. You're gone in three generations, and nobody cares. Before you showed up, nobody cared. It's all single-player."

Ask yourself:

> What game have I been playing lately that isn't mine? What would my life look like if I played by my own rules starting today?

When Naval refers to single-player games, he means that our life experiences, interpretations, and memories are uniquely our own and that, ultimately, we are responsible for defining and navigating our path. We determine what has meaning, and we do that through single-player games, not multi-player ones. This does not mean that we become individualistic people without care for our neighbors, community, families, etc. It just means they do not dictate the life we design for ourselves.

What Ravikant is pointing to is that in a single-player game, we have the agency to give meaning to our passion. Only us. It's a personal venture we must lean into, and accept any repercussions of. Multiplayer games keep us in the Drama Triangle, most likely stuck in the victim phase, where we think life is happening to us and not for us.

When we view life as a single-player game, we can see ourselves as the primary player rather than a pawn. Single-player games strip us of that very illusion. They give us back the power; they help us build our characters through our singular adversities and the ways we drive ourselves forth to overcome them. These games are internal and reflective, focusing on personal growth and well-being. Ideally, we come to learn that the only competition we are in is with ourselves.

The key is to consciously choose which games to play and to define what winning means for us as individuals. In the journey to design our ideal life, we'll face pressures from various sources like family, friends, colleagues, and society at large. These voices can be loud and persuasive, urging us to conform to conventional expectations. But we can choose which voice to listen to, the external opinions or our inner voice.

A core tenet of the single-player game is complete ownership of our decisions and outcomes, taking responsibility for the choices we make, both good and bad. It prompts us to ask ourselves how we contribute to the success or dysfunction of our life design. Where in our lives are we passively letting things unfold, and where are we actively taking ownership?

This whole process is about recognizing the power we have on our own path, even when there are gut-wrenching decisions to make. We've got to own the decisions that got us where we are today while also having the courage to make bold choices that push us toward the life we envision. It's so easy to blame the world, but the moment we take accountability for how our actions and reactions are shaping our reality, we can redefine what it means to take action and play a game that actually makes us feel like we're winning.

Once we know the role we're playing, we can get out of our own way and create the life we desire instead of staying stuck in any one particular stage of change or an old set of beliefs. Self-sabotage is a barrier that makes our BS Meters go haywire, leading to behaviors that undermine our progress. We can use our awareness of the ANS to shift from stress-driven reactions to a calmer, more focused state. When we feel overwhelmed or anxious, we now know it's often the sympathetic nervous system at work, signaling fight or flight. Recognizing this, we can actively engage the parasympathetic nervous system to regain clarity and control through self-care. By calming the nervous system, we create space for authentic choices. Remember:

> *Drama leads to stress which leads to negative outcomes which leads to costs.*

It'd be a shame to keep paying the cost, knowing what we know now. If the ANS governs our stress responses, then we know well how self-sabotage triggers a dysregulated system, often rooted in self-judgment and a lack of safety. But with that knowing comes the opportunity to make conscious, alternative choices that recalibrate our system instead of overloading it with garbage that is not rooted in truth.

When we decide to opt out of society's default game, we open ourselves up to the freedom of designing a life that fits us individually. We ask deeper questions about what brings us joy, fulfillment, and peace, rather than simply conforming to a societal script. In doing so, we start "playing" the games that matter most to us—games where our unique vision and personal values guide us. It lets us cultivate a life that's authentically ours, balancing aspirations with genuine fulfillment, instead of getting lost in someone else's vision of success.

So, instead of asking who we want to be, we need to ask ourselves what game we want to play.

Let's say you've been working through this book and have spent time creating your vision. You paused to reflect on the values that motivate you to keep moving toward the vision for your life. You have opened yourself up to your mode of brilliance, the passions that will drive you along the way to creating your ideal life. Well, now is where you'd say (to yourself), "Put me in, Coach. I'm ready to play. And I'm going to go at it alone. Just me and my superpowers within."

SETTING YOUR SINGLE-PLAYER GAME

Designing our ideal life is ongoing and ever-evolving, demanding patience, persistence, and a willingness to navigate the complexities of our human behavior and thought patterns. That's why understanding our relationship to change is so important. We can't create a life that truly aligns with our values if we're not willing to take control of our responses to change and actively shape our path forward. Games require strategy, intentional choices, self-awareness, and a commitment to playing by the rules or standards that serve our true vision.

We are in control of how we design our relationships, our community, and the social support systems that will serve as part of our game. Assessing the people we surround ourselves with and how they fit into our journey is key to shaping our environment in a way that helps us thrive. We can control how much or how little of cultural norms we choose to adopt, recognizing that while collective culture is important, it doesn't dictate our game.

Playing a single-player game doesn't mean detaching from others or disregarding the need for community. It's about creating the kind of support network that helps us stay safe, trusted, and focused on our passions, and having the courage to let go of people, places, and things that don't encourage that. In a single-player game, psychological safety enables us to fully express ourselves, take risks, and step into environments where our true vision can come to life. It's about designing a supportive and empowering space for our dreams, where others are present but do not dictate the rules. All of that is within our control to cultivate.

The game plan needs to revolve around our standards, our set of rules, and the foundations for our actions—much of which we have touched on in this book. But it requires a continuous cycle of listening, acting, and reflecting. Listening means tuning in to our inner voice, the one that knows what truly makes us happy and fulfilled. Acting involves taking deliberate steps toward our vision, even when those steps feel uncertain or risky. Reflecting means pausing to assess our progress, learning from our experiences, and adjusting our path as needed.

The single-player game is about mastering ourselves, our passions, and our emotions. Personal growth—whether in knowledge, skills, or emotional intelligence—becomes the focus of the game. This process requires a commitment to continuous learning and self-improvement, where we dedicate time and energy to improving our abilities without competing with others. In a single-player game, we stop seeking validation from others, whether from family, peers, or society. While relationships and community are important, they should not shape our choices.

Imagine logging into the game of life each day. The loading screen fades, and there we are, standing at the starting point of a brand-new level. But before we set out, before we take a single step, we've got to check our character stats. These include:

- Our ANS. That's our stamina bar. Are we feeling regulated, safe, and steady? Or is our system already on edge, ready to fight, flee, or freeze at the first obstacle?
- Our safety and trust. That's our shield. It protects our energy from draining too quickly.
- Our vision and values. Those are our quest logs, the purpose that gives our journey direction.
- Our self-care. That's our health potion, our way to replenish when the battles get tough.

These are our superpowers, the internal strengths that shape how we move through the game. We don't have to earn them because they're already within us, but we do need to know where we stand each time we log in.

Once our stats are checked, it's time to choose our one essential tool: our Sword of Superpowers. This is the only thing we need in our inventory because it's the tool that cuts through illusions, distractions, and drama. It's the tool we use to say no when something isn't aligned. It's the same tool that lets us say yes with an open heart, even when we're scared. The sword is our protector and our guide, but it's not about swinging wildly, but about knowing when to strike and when to hold.

And that's where our strategy comes in. The EAR Framework is the map we follow. Empathy keeps us from attacking when we need to listen. Accountability reminds us that this is our game, our choices, our moves, our consequences. Resilience helps us reset when we've lost a life, taken a hit, or found ourselves on a level we didn't expect.

These elements create a complete loadout for our single-player game. They help us stay grounded, aware, and intentional as we navigate every level, every challenge, and every opportunity.

Our job isn't to win against others. It's to win our own game, to master our vision, and to build a life designed by us, for us, with our truth at the center. Listening to our intuition is an act of courage and trust here. Joseph Campbell's concept of "following your bliss" speaks to this idea. The pursuit of bliss isn't frivolous, but it's also not straightforward. It needs a guiding post, and our intuition is the inner compass. It's the thing that, once we follow, helps us discern truth from deception. But to use this compass, we must be willing to assess and face the uncomfortable truths that come up along the way. Only then will unexpected doors open and opportunities emerge, ones we might never have imagined before.

So, do you feel worthy of following your bliss? Even if you don't feel it yet, you are worthy of designing a life that feels true to who you are, and no drama can stand in the way of that. Not even you, if you let your intuition guide you.

That requires addressing our limitations head-on. Sometimes, we find ourselves thrown into a situation where we don't get to pick the bucket of our lives we've got to focus on. It's in those moments, though, that the real work begins. Even if the change is forced, it's an invitation to reassess and step into our vision.

This is where the magic lies, in the moments of discomfort and uncertainty. That's where we get to decide if we're going to stay stuck in our BS and drama or follow the truth of our vision, no matter what the circumstances look like. The choice is ours, and it's one we are more than capable of making.

WHO ARE YOU BECOMING? DESIGNING WITH HABITS AND IDENTITY

One of the most empowering ways to take control of our life design is by focusing on who we want to become rather than just setting outcome-based goals. This approach taps into what James Clear calls "identity-based habits" in his book Atomic Habits. The science behind this concept is rooted in how our brains create neural pathways, turning repeated actions into efficient mental "shortcuts." This is why certain behaviors can become automatic, whether they support our growth or hold us back. The key is to shape these shortcuts to serve the person we aim to be.

Start small. Ask:

What does my ideal self look like, even in a single area of my life?

Say you want to be more resilient. Instead of pushing yourself to become instantly resilient in every situation, begin with small daily practices that embody resilience. Perhaps each night, you reflect on one challenge from your day and note how you handled it. Or when setbacks arise, try replacing frustration with curiosity: What can this teach me?

Each time we practice this, our brain reinforces this resilient identity, making it feel more natural over time. Remember, habits built around our desired identity will ultimately form the foundation for larger, transformative changes in our lives.

In *Positive Intelligence*, Shirzad Chamine introduces the idea that we all have inner "Saboteurs" and a "Sage" mind. Our Saboteurs represent the negative voices in our heads. These are deeply ingrained patterns of thought that often originate from our past experiences, self-criticism, or societal conditioning. They are part of our brain's survival wiring. They arise from the limbic system, particularly the amygdala, which is responsible for the fight, flight, or freeze responses that are triggered by perceived threats.

The Saboteurs emerge as mental shortcuts, helping us react quickly in situations that our brains interpret as risky or uncomfortable. Over time, these responses become habitual as our brains create neural pathways that strengthen with repetition. So, if we frequently tell ourselves we're "not good enough" or avoid hard conversations out of fear, these pathways solidify, making it easier to default to these negative patterns.

On the other hand, our Sage mindset embodies our best self.

The Sage operates from a place of calm, curiosity, empathy, and creativity rather than from fear or judgment.

Ask yourself:

- Which voice has been louder this week, my Saboteur or my Sage?
- What's one thing my Sage wants me to know right now?

Unlike Saboteurs, which are reactive, the Sage is proactive and solution-focused, allowing us to respond to situations with clarity rather than stress or impulsiveness. When we learn to activate our Sage, we foster resilience and approach challenges with an openness to learning and growth, not merely survival.

The Sage engages the prefrontal cortex, the part of the brain associated with higher-order functions like problem-solving, empathy, and rational decision-making. This is where we experience a sense of control and clarity, and it's also where we cultivate our capacity for creative thinking, curiosity, and compassion. Activating the Sage involves rewiring the brain by consciously choosing responses that counteract the default reactions of the Saboteurs. By repeatedly practicing these alternative responses, we create new neural pathways that can become as automatic as our Saboteur responses.

As Joseph Campbell said:

> "You must give up the life you planned in order to have the life that is waiting for you."

LIFE DESIGN IN ACTION: THE NEXT MOVE IS YOURS

To achieve this, we must shift away from rigid, fear-based thinking and learn to trust our Sage. Designing our lives is not about rigidly following a single blueprint but about learning to live with intention and flexibility, guided by the wisdom of our Sage.

This is also where we adjust the lens we've been taught to look through. Most of us have been conditioned to see life design as a one-size-fits-all model: work hard, achieve, earn, prove. But we get to question that. We get to decide how much of our life—whether it's all of it, some of it, or just a small piece—we want to design with intention. We get to ask:

- Which part of my superpowers needs attention right now?
- Am I following my values or someone else's blueprint?

Our other superpowers—our nervous system, our vision and values, our self-care, our sense of safety and trust—they're all working together in this. They give us the tools to recognize when we're slipping back into old patterns and help us reorient toward what's real and what matters most.

This is the heart of life design: knowing we can't control everything, but we can proactively design our lives to the extent that we can. It's about identifying the places where we get tripped up, where fear, doubt, or the Saboteurs take over, and pulling ourselves back into our vision and values. That's where change really happens.

Our life design is a practice. It's a continual process of tuning in, adjusting, and showing up for the life we're here to live. Our lives, not someone else's. Ask:

> What part of your "planned life" am I willing to release in order to access the one that's calling you?

CHAPTER 6:

Activate Contentment – The Crown Jewel

"I am a naked man, standing inside a mine of rubies, clothed in red silk."

— Rumi

"The small ruby everyone wants has fallen out on the road.
Some think it is east of us, others west of us.
Some say, 'among the primitive earth rocks,' others, 'in the deep waters.'
Kabir's instinct told him it was inside, and what it was worth,
and he wrapped it up carefully in his heart cloth."

— Kabir

This chapter is about that small ruby. Not the fleeting shine of pleasure, but the grounded radiance of contentment, wrapped carefully in the heart cloth.

From the time I sat down to write the first sentences of this book until now, I have changed. Not because something particularly major has occurred in my life, but because my life is a revolving door of circumstances, experiences, emotions, and memories that keep me evolving. Your life is, too, even if you feel like the door has been stuck for ten years and you can't seem to come up with the finances, or the time, or the motivation to fix it. You are evolving in some way. We all are.

As a society, we are in a constant state of developing, innovating, and overcoming circumstances. Our human ingenuity has continually found ways to solve problems. We accumulate knowledge and build on those past insights to create a foundation for future progress. This applies to all political, cultural, and social constructs. We are inevitably adapting every day, no matter how much we resist or refuse it or what side of the spectrum we're on. We are, collectively and individually, ever-evolving creatures. There is some faith to be had in inevitable progress.

Amidst the fear and uncertainty of riding the inevitable waves of those changes, we do our best to seek the happy moments. We look for the circumstances, achievements, relationships, or experiences that bring us joy or pleasure. We need them. We deserve them. We deserve to feel good.

In the words of poet Mary Oliver:

> "You do not have to be good.
> You do not have to walk on your knees
> for a hundred miles through the desert repenting.
> You only have to let the soft animal of your body
> love what it loves."

Humans experience pleasure differently from other animals. Neuroscientists have studied how our brains need those conscious moments of liking, wanting, and learning something that makes us feel pleasure. Pleasure is a fundamental component of happiness, and moments of happiness alleviate some of the suffering that comes with being human.

The "pursuit of happiness" is central to the U.S. vernacular, and a whole industry of books, retreats, and coaching practices is set up around this pursuit. In some ways, even this book and the work I do in the world could be encompassed in this "happiness genre." Yet the very expression also illustrates a paradox of that worldview: Perhaps when one pursues happiness too single-mindedly, one fails to notice and take advantage of what one already has.

In other words, striving for ever-greater happiness may set one on a hedonic treadmill to nowhere. A more grounded approach is to focus on making the most of what's available in the present before racing toward the future. But what exactly does "maximize what's available in the present" mean? It's not about squeezing every moment dry in a frenzy of productivity or pleasure but about being fully awake to the life unfolding in real time. Happiness often hides in the quiet, unremarkable spaces, sharing a meal, a deep conversation, the way the light hits our favorite corner of the room. When we pause to truly experience those moments, we create a foundation of contentment that isn't contingent on external achievements or future outcomes. And contentment is not the same as happiness.

THE REALIZATION THAT HAPPINESS IS NOT ENOUGH

I know it might sound indulgent to say that happiness is not enough, but hear me out. Happiness is about feeling good in the moment. It's a short-term or fleeting emotion or feeling dependent on a momentary circumstance. It is a state of well-being rooted in the external. It is one piece of the puzzle, often met with opposing emotions and feelings that combat it (and sometimes win). Sometimes, sadness, frustration, stress, and fear come swooping in through that revolving door, too.

I present that positive progress is found through a state of contentment, not happiness. Contentment isn't passive acceptance or forced gratitude. It's a stable internal baseline, a nervous system state of regulated awareness that holds steady when happiness and pain come and go. It's peace that doesn't depend on outcomes.

Through contentment, we find peace even amidst the BS that knocks us off our happy train. Through contentment, we get to focus on the puzzle as a whole, a mosaic where we question what happens, like the farmer and the horse story. We can find our state of satisfaction and ease because through contentment, we are grounded, stable, and feel safe in our bodies.

Happiness is often tied to external benchmarks, things we think will bring us joy, like buying a new car, getting a promotion, or going on a trip. We believe that these moments of pleasure will lead to lasting fulfillment. This is known as the hedonistic treadmill. We chase one pleasure after another, thinking each will bring us lasting happiness, but we always end up back at the same place. No matter how many times we hop on that treadmill, it keeps going, but the satisfaction never truly lasts.

Contentment, however, is different. Contentment is a state of mind, not a feeling that comes from external achievements. While happiness is an emotion we experience in response to specific events, contentment is about finding peace with where we are, even in the face of difficulty. Life is hard, and there will always be suffering, but learning to accept that and still find joy in the little moments is where true well-being lies.

The thing about pleasure is that it's temporary. It's human nature to enjoy things, but over time, that pleasure fades as we get used to whatever it is we've acquired. A new house, a new car, or a new relationship all bring a rush of joy at first, but that joy gradually wears off. It's not just pleasure that fades over time. Even the pain of a setback or loss, like a break-up or bad diagnosis, also dulls with time. It's part of how our brains are wired to adapt.

This is why it's so important to seek contentment instead of chasing after happiness. Contentment is grounded in the ability to stay present, appreciate what we have, and know that it's okay when the rush of excitement or sadness fades. When we accept that pleasure will eventually fade and that life will always involve its ups and downs, we can learn to savor the moments as they come, while also keeping our feet firmly grounded in a state of contentment.

I've learned that contentment isn't about avoiding pain or seeking constant pleasure; it's about finding a stable, inner peace that allows us to navigate life's challenges without constantly chasing after happiness. This is the real work of being an adult: learning how to accept both the highs and the lows, and finding a way to stay rooted in a state of contentment despite it all. When we focus on finding purpose and meaning in our lives, contentment becomes the steady ground we return to, no matter what happens around us. This becomes the practice of standing firm and grounded, finding satisfaction in the present moment, and knowing that no matter what comes our way, we'll be okay.

When we learn to stop chasing the emotional high and fearing the low, we open ourselves to something more sustainable. Not numbness, not indifference, just a steady presence. This is the powerful art of neutrality.

MAKE LIKE SWITZERLAND & FIND YOUR NEUTRAL

Life often feels like a constant push-and-pull between extremes. One moment, we're up, basking in the glow of success or joy, and the next, we're down, caught in the throes of pain or disappointment. We chase after happiness, trying to find the next big thing that will bring us lasting contentment. But what if true peace isn't found in the highs and lows, but in the steady middle ground?

Think about the Chinese farmer and how his response to life's ever-changing events, "Maybe so, maybe not," captures the essence of neutrality. His wisdom lies in accepting that life's ups and downs are not inherently good or bad. They simply are. When we learn to let go of our attachment to outcomes, we free ourselves from the constant rollercoaster of pleasure and pain. We preserve our energy for what truly matters: contentment in the face of it all.

Our ANS is a key tool in our pursuit of neutrality. It's the part of us that dictates how we react to life's pressures, whether we're in fight-or-flight mode or in a state of calm and connection. We don't have to be at the mercy of the automatic reactions that might make us catastrophize, jump to conclusions, or want to give up. We can learn to work with our ANS, using its responses to guide us toward balance instead of reacting impulsively to every emotional shift.

When we tap into our ventral vagal system, we can stay grounded even in turbulent moments. By engaging with it, we teach ourselves to slow down, breathe, and respond from a place of calm, rather than reacting with anxiety or stress. This is how we stay centered. Not by trying to avoid challenges or pretending the lows don't exist, but by recognizing them and choosing how to respond with equanimity.

When we stop attaching so strongly to the highs and lows of life, we don't get tossed around as much. When we stay neutral, we're able to experience life's pleasures more fully, because we know they won't last forever, and that's okay. But when things get tough, we don't crumble under the weight of adversity, because we understand that hardship, too, is temporary.

The goal is not to eliminate the ups and downs but to create a space in between where we don't get swept away. This is how we stay in the flow. This is how we create sustainability in our emotional lives. We must activate our personal agency and choose to remain steady, no matter the storm.

CHECK YOUR PROJECTIONS

When things in my life are going well, I can easily drift into the outer aspects of life. When things start to fall apart, that is often when I feel the strong pull to get introspective. It's during these times of introspection that true change can occur. As Moshe Feldenkrais said:

> "You can't change what you're doing until you know what you're doing."

Reaching contentment requires the recognition of our predictability in times of turmoil. It asks us to call out the patterns that evoke judgment, impulse, and extreme emotional reactions from us. To reach contentment is to have transcendental awareness. It is to be in a state of consciousness that goes beyond everyday thoughts and feelings. It is a heightened state of awareness where we are so deeply connected to something bigger than ourselves and the drama (which we'll talk more about), that we can always find our clarity and peace. To get there and stay there, we've got to know what pulls us out of that state to begin with.

We're all projecting something—good, bad, or apathetic. Projection is merely a defense mechanism we use to victimize ourselves by placing the blame on others. If someone feels insecure about their abilities at work, they might be quick to accuse others of being judgmental or critical of them because they're already judging themselves. If someone holds onto shame or guilt, they might be quick to assume others are judging them as if they've done something wrong because they already think they did.

Projection causes drama and leads to more conflict, but it also keeps us in our comfort zones by allowing us to avoid confronting uncomfortable truths about ourselves, our own private BS. When we project, we sidestep the work of adults. We tell ourselves false narratives about who we are and how safe we are (or aren't) in our environments, which triggers an unfavorable reaction.

It's important to pay close attention to our habitual, well-conditioned reactions. We need to be honest about whether our feelings and beliefs are simply projections of our own unchecked emotions or if they genuinely reflect our core values and virtues. Recognizing this helps us avoid drama and face the root of our internal struggles rather than projecting them onto our external reality. When we recognize the root cause of our reactions, we can work through them constructively and stabilize ourselves.

What I'm saying is: Get used to calling yourself out on your BS. Get used to taking accountability for how you react and learn from the behavior so you can choose a different path. That different path is where you find contentment: The Middle Path. It's where you become better equipped to handle the ups and downs without being swayed by those emotions you haven't actually dealt with.

LET YOUR EAR BE YOUR GUIDE

Contentment doesn't happen overnight. It's not something we simply arrive at after a short sprint. It's more like a garden:

sometimes we water it, and other days, the weeds grow faster than the flowers. That's okay. The key is showing up consistently, even when things feel off course. This is a practice. I promise, no one will close this book and suddenly become a zen master of self-control. We all stumble, fumble, and have facepalm moments along the way. But that's part of the gig.

You've probably heard the classic Mike Tyson quote before:

"Everyone has a plan until they get punched in the face."

Life is going to throw us curveballs. There will be days when we feel like we're riding the wave of contentment, and others when the current pulls us under. But the practice of maintaining balance through it all comes from consistency, and that's where the EAR framework can help. These three pillars keep us aligned with the life we want to create, even when external circumstances don't cooperate. Here's how I want us to think about this:

- **Meet Yourself Where You're At (Empathy):** When life derails us, when things feel out of balance, it's easy to start judging ourselves for "falling off the path" or "not being good enough." Empathy asks us to pause and soften, to work to understand our internal state with compassion. When we feel anxious, frustrated, or exhausted, empathy is the part of us that says, "What's really going on here?" Rather than asking "What's wrong with me?" empathy lets us ask "What do I need?"
- **Show Up For Yourself (Accountability):** This is where the rubber meets the road. We cannot beat ourselves up or shame ourselves for falling short. That's when we need to bring out that BS Meter and call ourselves out. This process is about owning our choices and behaviors and asking, "What am I choosing right now?" It's about realizing that we always have the power to choose how we respond to life's challenges. When our plan is derailed or life feels too heavy,

accountability gives us the clarity to ask, "Is this response aligned with the person I want to be?" It helps us recalibrate in the moment instead of spiraling or staying stuck.

- **Come Back, Again and Again (Resilience):** I'm not talking about the kind of resilience that tells us to push through or "just deal with it." I'm talking about the kind of resilience that allows us to fall apart and rise again, over and over, as many times as we need. It's the resilience that understands that life's challenges will knock us down, but we can always come back up, a little stronger, a little wiser. Resilience focuses on knowing when to rest, recalibrate, and start fresh. It's about accepting that hardship is part of the human experience, and that we can navigate it with grace, even when it feels impossible.

As long as we show up, consistently returning to our inner compass (our vision and values), we will be able to realign and find our center, no matter how life derails us. We'll find ourselves moving toward neutrality, steady in the face of life's ups and downs. This is how we nurture contentment. Not by chasing happiness, but by showing up, time and time again, for the life we're building.

UPDATE YOUR BRAIN'S REWARD SYSTEM

We all know dopamine as the "feel-good" neurotransmitter. It's pivotal to our brain's reward system, influencing our pleasure, motivation, and reinforcement of our behaviors. It helps us learn from and repeat actions that bring us some sort of pleasure or reward.

Dopamine heavily impacts our cognitive functioning. Whether that occurs in a negative or positive way, though, is up to us. Our brains are wired to chase reward, and the world offers no shortage of ways to stay overstimulated. But contentment requires intention. That means recalibrating how we choose to pursue pleasure. It starts by noticing what gives us a real sense of ease, and what leaves us depleted. It begins with assessing which behaviors lead to calm, and which pull us into chaos. Dopamine isn't the problem. It's how we earn it that matters. The goal isn't to quit pleasure. It's to retrain our system to crave what actually sustains us. It's the age-old adage:

> "We buy shit we don't need, with money we don't have, to impress people we don't like."

And all of it imbalances our dopamine levels.

Excessive stimulation of dopamine pathways creates a cycle of seeking constant reward and leads to an overstimulated dopamine system. Over time, we become desensitized to dopamine's effects, which leads to less pleasure, which causes us to find more intense (and often unhealthy) forms of stimulation to achieve some level of satisfaction. This is the plight of substance abuse. On the flip side, if these behaviors lead to burnout, stress, or poor mental health, we deplete our dopamine and weaken our system altogether. From there, it's fatigue, depression, lack of motivation, and driving up cravings for all the quick fixes. Or worse, leading to more manic behaviors and addiction.

Not all rewards are good rewards. We wouldn't hand a diabetic a bag of candy to congratulate them for a job well done. We wouldn't reward someone's sobriety with a cocktail. So, ask:

> Where am I getting my dopamine? And how am I prioritizing its balance?

Balanced dopamine levels come from having enjoyable experiences without becoming dependent on them for constant stimulation. Proper exercise, diet, and sleep are foundational aspects of maintaining healthy dopamine levels. Working toward and achieving personal goals, reaffirming ourselves, having positive social interactions in safe environments, and engaging in activities that challenge our brains all contribute to balanced dopamine. The goal is to create healthy, sustainable habits over unhealthy, quick fixes.

Like all systems, there needs to be updating on occasion. This means reviewing and reevaluating the activities and the people we engage with. It requires us to ask things like:

- Who has access to me? And why?
- Who and what is truly adding value to my life?

These are within our control. What worked well in the past might need modification to remain effective. When we notice persistent dissatisfaction that is met with a form of stimulation that does not serve our growth, it might be time to make adjustments. We cannot be content unless we are proactive about adjusting our behaviors and reactions accordingly.

HOLD CLOSE YOUR BS METER

I think of Laurie Anderson, an avant-garde artist and artistic philosopher who often addresses themes related to the human condition. She says that there are three rules to live by. The first is not to be afraid of anyone. Fear of others, whether due to opinions, status, or power, limits our authenticity. We must approach life with courage. Overcoming those fears is what gives us the freedom to live authentically. When we're not constrained by external noise, we can pursue our passions, set boundaries, and live true to who we are.

The second is to get a good BS detector and learn how to use it. We've got to be able to recognize dishonesty, manipulation, or insecurity in all aspects of our lives. By developing a strong sense of discernment, we can make informed decisions and navigate interactions with a clear mind.

How close to or how far from the BS am I?

When we know the answer to that question, we are less likely to be ensnared by negative influences or problematic dynamics that make up all the drama.

The last is to be tender. Without compassion and empathy toward ourselves and others, we cannot foster meaningful relationships or personal well-being. We are all seeking a sense of belonging and connection, all of which are crucial for lasting contentment. This goes back to Carl Rogers's concept of unconditional positive regard. The idea is holding space for each other—flaws, fears, and all—without judgment.

It's not so much about fixing or saving as it is about seeing someone fully and saying, "I'm here, and you matter." And that includes ourselves. Too often, we extend kindness outward but neglect the person in the mirror. Tenderness isn't weakness; it's the courage to show up authentically, to honor the messy, imperfect humanity that binds us all. Imagine how our relationships and our lives might transform if we dared to embrace this kind of radical compassion. Wouldn't that be something worth striving for?

As I mentioned at the beginning, and several times throughout this work, all drama begins and ends with us. This means that, no matter what external circumstances we face, the choices we make within ourselves shape the outcome. Drama is often a product of where we choose to place our energy. Feeding into the BS instead of investing in our authenticity is a choice. When we choose fear, dishonesty, and the avoidance of tenderness, we perpetuate drama. But when we choose courage, clarity, and compassion, both for ourselves and others, we disrupt the cycle of chaos.

This isn't about avoiding conflict or pretending everything is perfect. That's just not logical. But it is about creating a foundation where we can approach challenges with a clear mind and a grounded heart. That's logical. When we choose to act from a place of authenticity, when we honor our boundaries and embrace tenderness, we create the conditions necessary for true connection, both within ourselves and with others. This shifts us from a state of drama to one of meaningful engagement. It's in this space, where fear, dishonesty, and resistance no longer hold sway, that we find the room to grow, heal, and thrive.

Now would be a good time to ask yourself:

"What is my role in the success or dysfunction of how the drama operates in my life?"

This question cuts to the heart of everything we've been exploring. It forces us to take radical accountability, not in a way that blames or shames but in a way that empowers. When we acknowledge our role in either feeding the chaos or fostering clarity, we reclaim our agency. It's a reminder that we're not just passive recipients of the drama around us. We're participants, and more importantly, we're capable of change.

By identifying how we contribute—through fear, dishonesty, or resistance—we can begin to dismantle those patterns and choose authenticity, courage, and tenderness instead. This isn't about control over others or external circumstances. It's about mastering ourselves and deciding, once and for all, to stop being complicit in our own discontentment.

SURRENDER TO SOMETHING HIGHER THAN YOU

Finding enduring contentment starts with knowing ourselves, what we value, what brings us joy, and what drains our energy. It's rooted in taking care of our foundations, our bodies, minds, and spirits. When we nourish, move, and rest, we create space for something deeper to emerge: a sense of trust in our ability to weather life's storms. Contentment is the fruit-bearing tree. Its roots run deep, securing it through the elements. Even when storms rage and branches sway, the tree knows it has what it needs to remain upright and continue bearing fruit.

But what happens when the storm feels insurmountable, when everything we thought we knew about balance and stability is stripped away? I recognize this will absolutely happen. God knows I've been there. That's where surrender comes in, a lesson I've learned the hard way and one I continue to revisit. Surrendering is about releasing the illusion of control and trusting in something greater than ourselves. Whether we call it divine intelligence, a higher power, or simply the flow of life, surrendering is what allows us to move forward, even in the face of unimaginable pain.

In October 2021, I vividly remember having a true moment of complete and utter happiness. I was on my way to work with a beautiful resort the very next day, going to school to improve my skill set, and feeling balanced, like my life was in harmony. And then, two days after arriving at what felt like paradise, I got the call: my dad was sick with COVID. Within 48 hours, my world flipped. The yin and yang of happiness and sorrow collided in a way I'd never experienced before, forcing me to confront life's impermanence. And three weeks later, I lost my beloved father, the only true hero I've ever had in this life.

What followed in the wake of his passing was a lot of darkness. It was messy. It wasn't always graceful. I grieved deeply, felt lost, and grappled with emotions I didn't always know how to process. It was not the proudest period of my life, to say the least. I wasn't making choices that served me. I honestly felt I didn't know how to help myself, despite all the tools I had at my disposal and the work I had done throughout my life and career to that point.

But amid that devastation, I learned what it truly means to surrender and the true solace it has to offer. I had to let go, not just of my father, but of the fear, dishonesty, and resistance that kept me from moving through the pain. I realized that healing begins when we stop fighting the current and allow ourselves to be carried by it. Rich Roll often describes surrender as stepping out of our ego-driven need to control and into the higher intelligence that flows through us all. It's not about giving up but aligning with life's natural rhythms, even in chaos. Surrendering is the act of acknowledging that there is something greater at work, a force that carries us forward if we let it.

Gratitude became my anchor. Shifting focus to what I had, even in moments of profound loss, elevated me to a higher vibration. Sean Achor's Harvard research on gratitude shows how it rewires the brain, allowing us to see possibilities where we once saw despair. For me, gratitude meant being thankful for the time I had with my dad, for the lessons he taught me, and for the love we shared. That perspective didn't erase the pain, but it gave me a foundation to stand on, a root system for my tree. Gratitude shifted my gaze from what was broken to what was still whole.

Through grief, I found rebirth. I began asking deeper questions:

- What wasn't working in my life?
- What fears were holding me back?
- How could I father myself in his absence?

This process, painful as it was, led me to understand that contentment isn't about perfection or constant happiness. It's about standing resilient in the storm, rooted in the knowledge that we have what we need to endure.

Gratitude and surrender are companions, walking hand in hand. Together, they form a path through even the darkest times. Gratitude reminds us of life's gifts, even in suffering, while surrender teaches us to trust the flow of life. Neither is easy, but both are essential. Surrendering didn't mean avoiding the pain; it meant sitting with it, letting it teach me, and ultimately finding clarity. That clarity rewired my perspective, helped me downregulate my nervous system, and brought me closer to what truly matters.

The concepts in this book are solid lifelines born from lived experience, evidence-based research, and the wisdom of others who've walked similar paths. Surrender and gratitude hold it all together. They provide the doorway to contentment that's not just fleeting but enduring. And they keep us in our state of kindness, too.

BE THE KINDNESS

Kindness is not a soft, passive act. It is not something that happens when it's convenient or when the path is easy. True kindness, the kind that sustains and nourishes, requires a certain level of strength, courage, and conscious effort. It's about choosing compassion over judgment, peace over drama, and, most importantly, showing up even when it's difficult.

In the face of life's unpredictability and challenges, kindness is our anchor. It's the thread that runs through the Six Superpowers, the glue that holds everything together. Without it, our best intentions become hollow, our self-care becomes narcissistic, and our agency shifts into control, disconnected from compassion. Kindness doesn't just make life better, it makes life work.

The world around us is constantly calling us to react, to dive into the drama, to match the noise with our own. But kindness is the powerful antidote to this chaos. It doesn't force us to try and avoid conflict or pretend things are fine when they're not. Kindness is about meeting life with honesty, vulnerability, and courage. It's about wielding a Sword of Superpowers to see through the illusions and the fear that often cloud our judgment.

Think of that sword as our weapon of mass kindness. It allows us to say "no" when necessary, but with the same fierce love that we say "yes" to life. It helps us navigate uncomfortable conversations with grace, and it enables us to hold our ground when everything around us seems to be pulling us off-center. With this sword, we don't fight to dominate; we fight to preserve our peace, our authenticity, and our values.

In a world that constantly pulls us toward drama, being kind—truly kind—is an act of rebellion. It's choosing to rise above the petty disagreements, the negativity, and the gossip that often cloud our minds. It's an intentional, strategic choice, one that grounds us in our values, anchors us in our purpose, and brings us back to contentment.

When we make kindness our default, it becomes the lever that amplifies every other superpower within us. It stabilizes our nervous system, builds deep trust in our relationships, and helps us stay steady when the storm hits. It turns difficult situations into opportunities for growth, and it makes space for authentic connection. Kindness works. It creates a ripple effect that extends far beyond our own lives.

This is why I say to be the kindness. It's not something we should do just when it's easy. It's a practice, a muscle that gets stronger the more we use it. When we make kindness our strategy, it will lead us home to contentment, because kindness doesn't drain us; it replenishes us. It is the antidote to chaos and the source of true peace.

So, I compel you to pick up your sword and hold it with intention. Let it guide you through the tumult. Choose kindness, not as a reaction, but as your way of being. Let it be the quiet strength that keeps you content and at peace, no matter what life throws your way. When you embody kindness, everything else falls into place. Don't believe me? Just try!

Reactivate! Repetition is the Mother of Learning

"I'm not out to change the world, only my response to the world. And that changes everything."

— Eric Stephenson

There was a specific defining moment in my life when I thought, "I really believe my iPhone has a soul." I mean, listen to this story and see if there is any other way to explain it.

I befriended Jerry when we were both in the midst of our time as professional musicians. He was a mellow, good-hearted funk guitarist who idolized Prince. I was a mellow, good-hearted, rock guitarist who wanted to be Edward Van Halen. We both taught guitar lessons at a local music studio, and even though our musical tastes were worlds apart, we became fast friends.

Soon after meeting, he broke up with his long-term girlfriend of eight years. Or, to put it more correctly, she ended their relationship abruptly. His world was wrecked. My heart really ached for the guy. We grew closer as I became not only his shoulder to cry on but also his stand-in therapist.

I noticed that as his heart healed and got beyond the need to talk incessantly through the small cracks and crevices of his broken love affair, our conversations always seemed very one-sided in his favor.

We walked and talked through the joys and struggles of his life while I increasingly felt my needs weren't being met in the friendship. I wasn't invited to share what was going on in my life, and because of this feeling, I increasingly felt like I was checking out mentally when we were together. I started questioning if this was the right friendship for me, though I did not know how to take action. Or, perhaps, I was too cowardly to do so.

On a particular evening such as this, we were out having dinner, and I was really acutely aware of the imbalance once again in our conversations—his music, his successes, his struggles. As I grew weary, I had one beer, and then another, and then another to try to numb myself to the sensations of frustration and sadness welling up in me. I kept thinking, "This isn't a friendship, Eric. You're being sucked dry right now and feeling increasingly despondent."

I cannot explain what happened next, and I honestly believe some form of providence moved through my iPhone.

The next day, I was driving through town with my brother when he turned to me and asked, "How was your night with Jerry?"

I remember staring out the window of his SUV, saying, "You know, I love him like a brother, but every time we get together, I feel so drained during and afterward. He never really asks about what's going on in my life, and I end up listening to him talk the entire time." Then, I glanced down at my lap, and my iPhone was 45 seconds into a dialed call with... Guess who? It's true! OMG!!! Somehow my iPhone had dialed Jerry's number, and I wasn't sure if he might be on his phone listening to me, or if I went straight to voicemail, or maybe just maybe (through some miracle) the phone was still ringing on his end. I looked at my brother with a look of horror and quickly killed the call.

Three hours later, his name popped up on my screen as my phone rang out, spiking my cortisol levels as I completely froze. I couldn't find the courage to answer it. Minutes later, my voicemail alert showed up, and with a racing heart, I heard his voice pierce through me.

"Hi E, man, it was good to hang with you last night. But hey, I just got this really weird voicemail from you, and I think what you were saying may be about me. So please call me when you get this message." Click.

I coached myself for the next couple of hours, and at the end of it, decided it was time for me to be an adult and have a difficult conversation. A conversation long, long overdue.

When he picked up the phone, I started by saying, "Jerry, I need to say some things, and I really want to be as honest as I possibly can. I love you like a brother, but our friendship is not working for me." The protective armor finally fell off my heart's chest, and I spent the next 15 minutes describing exactly how I was feeling and what I thought about our friendship. When I was done, the phone fell quiet with a deafening silence.

Then, I heard him sobbing on the other end. "Every time we get together, I feel like all I'm doing is dumping on you, and I feel so guilty about it afterward. But honestly, you're the only one who really deeply listens to me. I am so, so sorry I have affected you the way I have. I am a terrible friend."

Then I began to sob.

We hung up the phone that day and never talked again. It was as if we said everything we needed to say to each other and then let go with love. I instantly felt an incredible sense of peace about it, and even though I miss him at times, I know our relationship had reached its end. The only lingering feeling I had was some guilt about not having an honest conversation with him sooner.

For me, this was a defining moment. It provided an emotional throughline that grounded me in themes of agency, boundaries, and compassion. The "iPhone call" was divine intervention illustrating what activation looks like in real time. And that activation is so hard.

Change is hard. It's easier to stay in situations that make us feel stuck, even when we know they are no longer good for us. But the truth is, change is inevitable. Whether we like it or not, life will present us with moments that force us to evolve. The key is how we respond to those moments.

Change is a process. It can feel messy and uncomfortable, and we may not always get it right the first time. But the more we go through cycles of change, the better we get at recognizing them. We start to notice patterns in how we react and, more importantly, how we can respond differently next time.

Life will always challenge us to grow. The question isn't whether change will come but how we'll respond when it does. With every cycle of change, we'll get better at embracing discomfort, taking action, and staying true to ourselves. The more we practice, the easier it gets to trust our ability to navigate change with authenticity.

Repetition is key, though. It's the process of showing up over and over, despite the messiness, mistakes, and obstacles. Through this, transformation unfolds. But to navigate the noise and distractions of the world, we need a solid defense, our most primal, utilitarian tool. The more we experience change, the better we get at handling it. It's not linear, and some days will be harder than others. But with each challenge, we grow stronger and more capable of facing the next.

KEEP CLOSE YOUR COMPASSION (AND YOUR BOUNDARIES)

Throughout this book, I have gone back to the Sword of Superpowers quite frequently. This is because I believe it becomes the perfect tool for the life we are fashioning in activating our personal agency. The sword allows us to shape our lives, our relationships, and our destinies with a deep commitment to the truth and a desire to free ourselves from the drama. It allows us to take action in a way that is aligned with our highest values, moving through the obstacles that prevent us from living fully and authentically.

In the words of spiritual teacher Jack Kornfield:

> "The courageous heart is the one that is unafraid to open to the world, to care no matter what. With compassion, we come to

trust our capacity to open to life without armoring. Compassion is not foolish. It doesn't just go along with what others want so they don't feel bad. There is a yes in compassion, and there is also a no, said with the same courage of heart. No to abuse, no to racism, no to violence, both personal and worldwide. The no is said not out of hate but out of an unwavering care. Buddhists call this the fierce sword of compassion. It is the powerful no of leaving a destructive family, the agonizing no of allowing an addict to experience the consequences of his acts."

This isn't just about kindness and compassion, but stepping fully into our power, our Six Superpowers within. The sword is a tool of clarity to keep us in our power, to use discernment, to claim agency over our lives. It protects our peace and honors our boundaries. It helps us take action from a place of integrity, not reactivity. It doesn't attack. It doesn't seek revenge. It says: "This is what I stand for. This is where I draw the line."

It channels:

- **Empathy,** to remain open without becoming overwhelmed.
- **Accountability,** to speak truth with compassion and clarity.
- **Resilience,** to show up again and again, even when it's uncomfortable.

This is not the sword of battle. It's the sword of awakening.

How we carry it defines how we show up—in leadership, in parenting, in partnership, and in the mirror. Whether we raise it in celebration, sever what no longer serves, or use it to protect what's sacred, this sword is ours to wield.

Some years ago, I was leading a fairly large workshop, sharing a vulnerable story about feeling personally disempowered. Suddenly, one participant made an inappropriate sexual comment. Without hesitation, I drew my metaphorical sword. I looked that person in the eyes, and I said, "If you or anyone else makes an inappropriate comment in this room, I will personally escort you out. Am I clear?"

The room fell silent.

Later, one participant came up to me and said, "I don't know what you just did, but it was powerful." It wasn't the sword itself, it was the boundaries I had set for myself and the unwavering commitment to respect at that moment. I would not stand for that type of behavior, and I held onto my sword with the fullest conviction.

In the deepest sense, I was the captain of the ship, ensuring my passengers were all psychologically safe. I owned that space, and if I had either ignored the comment or, even worse, laughed it off, I would have lost my power as the leader and consequently, the trust of the group. This is such a subtle but crucial point to emphasize. It's all about setting and maintaining safe and effective boundaries for all, and having the courage to take hold of an extremely hot flame.

Boundaries are the foundation of wielding the Sword of Superpowers effectively. They are the invisible lines we draw to define what is acceptable and what is not, both in how we treat others and how we allow ourselves to be treated. When our boundaries are clear, they serve as a signal to others that we value respect, integrity, and emotional safety. However, boundaries are not always easy to define or enforce. They require self-awareness, courage, and the willingness to risk discomfort in the pursuit of peace.

As a wise teacher once told me, we often only learn where boundaries are by crossing them or having something hurt us enough to know we need them. We mess up. We give too much, we allow too much, or we retreat too far. It's through this trial and error, this repetition, that we build resilience and understand our capacity for the BS. If we do what we've always done, we'll get what we've always gotten.

Lots of the concepts we've discussed in this book are part of the work for setting boundaries. For example:

- **Chapter One:** In any given situation, we have agency with three choices: change it, accept it, or end it.

- **Chapter Two:** We cannot remain stuck in situations, environments, or relationships that corrode the nature of our being and expect to feel safe. "Who has access to me and why?" Part of ensuring our safety is employing the right boundaries, separating what's genuine and what's toxic, and knowing when, where, and how our sword needs to be wielded.
- **Chapter Three:** Getting clear on our values and what matters most to us is key to setting healthy boundaries. Our time, energy, and emotional well-being deserve our utmost attention. That means knowing when and how to state our needs and limits assertively yet compassionately, leaving no room for ambiguity. In the words of the late rock legend Meatloaf: "I'll do anything for love, but I won't do that."
- **Chapter Four:** Re-evaluating and re-establishing our relationship with self-care is part of boundary building. Investing in ourselves and caring for our mind, body, and soul is learning when to invest in relationships or walk away and set limits heavily. Saying "no" to what doesn't serve us affirms our self-worth and reminds others of our value.
- **Chapter Five:** Life design is about intentionally creating a life that aligns with our values and vision. Boundaries are essential in this process because they protect our time, energy, and focus, ensuring that we don't get pulled into distractions that aren't aligned with your goals. Without boundaries, life design becomes reactive rather than intentional. When we design our lives with clear boundaries, we create space to nurture what matters most to us, whether it's relationships, creativity, or self-care.
- **Chapter Six:** Contentment is rooted in accepting where we are, but that doesn't mean passively accepting everything around us. Boundaries are key to contentment because they help us create an environment where peace can thrive. When

> we set boundaries—whether in relationships, work, or your internal dialogue—we protect your emotional and mental space, allowing room for calm and satisfaction. Boundaries help us stay grounded and prevent external chaos from disturbing our inner peace. By respecting our boundaries, we give ourselves permission to enjoy the present moment regardless of what's going on around us.

When we are honing these practices, drama loses its power. Drama relies on blurred lines and emotional reactions. It creates chaos by exploiting our uncertainty and feeding on our unresolved emotions. But when our boundaries are clear and firmly rooted, drama has no place to take hold. It can only thrive in environments where dysregulated nervous systems are running the show, where there's a lack of structure, or where people have no idea what their limits are. When we draw that Sword of Superpowers, we create a space where the only things that can flourish are respect and integrity.

ALLOW ME TO REPEAT MYSELF

The only thing the sword requires of us is consistency. It requires that we be disciplined in our practice to uphold our boundaries and reinforce our ability to draw the line effectively. There is a reason I repeat myself so much in this book. I have not reiterated my points to feed my writer's ego. I repeat myself because it's how we learn. We build on ourselves through practice, through reiteration, through our commitment to show up for our vision and values at every turn, over and over again, until it becomes second nature.

A student once said to his Zen master, "Teacher, you never lose your focused presence."

The master smiled and replied, "I lose it all the time. I just returned to it so quickly that you never notice."

The lesson? Mastery isn't about never losing balance; it's about repetition until it becomes second nature.

Repetition supports us in building the bulletproof self. Repetition builds resilience. The more we show up and practice, the more second-nature these tools become. Every day, we're making choices that define our lives. As we've discussed, drama is a product of stress and emotional reaction. Through the repetitive practice of emotional regulation, calming ourselves in the face of chaos by choosing the middle path, drama has little room to grow.

And the more aligned we are with our true selves, the less tolerance we'll have for drama and nonsense. That, my friends, is where true contentment lives.

Repeat the practices that align and draw that sword when necessary. Cut through the BS. It's not about escaping the mundane but mastering the art of showing up. Here are several ways we may wield the sword:

- **As a reminder of personal and professional boundaries:** The Sword of Superpowers serves as a silent reminder of our limits and what we will and will not tolerate, creating a safe space in our relationships and responsibilities. It helps u define our boundaries clearly: "I love you, and I'm willing to meet you halfway, but if you overstep that boundary, I'm out." It's the ultimate tool for protecting our peace while maintaining compassion.

- **As a symbol of victory:** There are moments when the gladiator takes the sword from the sheath, raises it high into the air, and exclaims, "Today we claim victory!" The CEO may congratulate the team for hitting their goals, the soccer coach for the team winning the division championship, or the parent for a child's recital performance. The sword is raised in the air, and the battle cry is: "Let's celebrate!"

- **As a tool for bestowing honor:** The sword can be used ceremonially to acknowledge someone's growth or contribution,"I knight you." It's a gesture of respect and love, bestowing honor with the same reverence as a sword tap on the shoulder.

- **As a blade to sever ties with people, places, and things:** Sometimes the sword must be used to cut ties with what no longer serves us. It's the act of saying, "I'm no longer willing to invest in this, and it will no longer live rent-free in my mind." This might mean ending a toxic relationship, letting go of addiction, or stepping away from harmful environments.
- **As a guiding force in parenting:** Using the Sword of Superpowers in parenting often means offering tough love or delivering hard truths when they are necessary for a child's growth. It's about balancing empathy with firm guidance to nurture their development in a psychologically safe environment.

I need you to go easy on yourself, though. I need you to go at this with the ambition of your inner child learning to ride a bike without training wheels for the first time. Go at this knowing that you are going to fall off the bike. Prepare for a boo-boo or three, buy your favorite band-aids with the superheroes on them, and know that eventually, through the process of repeated action, you will be riding in style.

YOUR INNER TEACHER WILL APPEAR

I can't let you go without addressing the paradox of control. In the last chapter, I discussed the importance of surrendering. I mentioned Rich Roll's views on stepping out of our ego-driven need to control and into the higher intelligence that flows through us all. The paradox lies in the fact that while we control very little of what goes on around us. At the same time, we hold complete responsibility and agency over our choices. It sounds contradictory, but it's true. The power lies in knowing where to let go and where to lean in.

And as I've emphasized, unless someone explicitly asks for my opinion or advice, I don't offer it. Why? Because unsolicited wisdom often falls flat. I don't know what's beyond your BS. It's like the old adage says:

"When the student is ready, the teacher will appear. When the student is truly ready, the teacher will disappear."

So, here's your invitation as we near the final pages of this book:

What is next for me in my life?

Take out a piece of paper and draw a line down the middle, creating two columns. Label one column "Optimal" and the other "Insane."

1. Pick an area of your life you want to focus on—your health, relationships, career, family, or anything else.
2. Under "Optimal," list everything that's working well. What feels aligned, functional, and supportive?
3. Under "Insane," be brutally honest. Write down what's not working. Where are you repeating the same patterns, expecting different results? Remember Einstein's (alleged) quote: *"Insanity is doing the same thing over and over and expecting different results."*

From here, we have a choice: Do we keep doing what we've always done and getting what we've always gotten? Or do we decide to shift our thoughts, actions, and behaviors toward something more optimal?

One reminder: there is no "right" way to do things. But there are *always* more *optimal* ways. While perfection is unattainable, striving for the optimal is worth the effort. Ask yourself:

- On a scale of 1 to 10, how regulated is my stress response?
- Where am I imposing drama on others?
- Am I open to a new way of doing things? What might that look like?

- What is my contribution to both the success and dysfunction in my life?
- Who has access to me and why? Should they?

Don't chase perfection, just pursue clarity, alignment, and authenticity. See beyond the drama, own your brilliance, and hold yourself accountable for what you allow into your life.

LET THE ACTIVATION BEGIN

As we come full circle, let's pause to reflect on the journey we've taken together. At its core, this book has been about reclaiming your agency, the ability to design a drama-free life rooted in authenticity and intentionality. It starts with self-awareness and personal accountability. The question now is:

What role are you playing in shaping your life's outcomes?

Remember, we are the architect of our life's design, and owning that truth is the foundation of contentment. Getting entangled in the drama triangle is, of course, another option.

Throughout this journey, we've explored the autonomic nervous system (ANS) as our internal compass, the seed from which our tree grows. It guides how we regulate emotions and respond to life's inevitable stressors. Our ANS isn't just biology; it's our anchor to balance and contentment. This step is imminently crucial and one that has been grossly overlooked by Western society at large. I have good company in this with Dr. Andrew Huberman plainly stating it oh so well:

> "What we need to do is start to figure out how we can, especially for the next generation of kids, how to teach them to regulate their nervous system. So that they recognize that pulse of adrenaline as placing them in a compromised position. We have to leverage the idea that being able to hear and listen hinges on

the ability to be calm. Therefore, the ability to be calm is crucial to hearing and listening, and hearing and listening are crucial to our advancement as individuals and as groups. The problem is- everyone has been trying to do this backwards. They've said we all have to get along. We have to cancel- cancel culture. We all have to listen to one another. And I think again, we have to start from the inside. We have to teach it physiologically. Now I don't have a master plan on how to do that. But until we can learn to regulate the self, I don't think we are going to get where we want to go as a culture."

Mic drop.

When we cultivate a sense of safety and neutrality through the roots of our tree, we create space to navigate life's highs and lows with clarity and resilience. Without a solid foundation, everything else becomes unstable. Safety and trust are the core of our ability to endure life's challenges and stand firm in the face of adversity.

Our vision and values are where everything begins to take shape, where the trunk of our tree begins to grow. When our actions align with our personal vision and values, we build a life that feels authentic and purposeful. The trunk supports the growth of the entire tree, just as our values provide structure and direction for our lives. Ask yourself:

Are my choices rooted in what truly matters to me?

Self-care acts as the branches, the extensions of our personal growth, reaching out and supporting everything else. Self-care is the vital practice that sustains us. It's not indulgent. It's necessary. Self-care is about designing routines that nourish our spirit, fortify our resilience, and sustain our well-being. Without proper self-care, even the best intentions falter. As we age, self-care becomes increasingly important. After forty, it can feel like a part-time job, but it's the key to staying grounded.

Designing our lives is like creating a unique blueprint, not following someone else's plan. These are our leaves. When we design our lives based on our vision and values, we build something that reflects who we truly are. Life design requires us to shift our focus from society's "multi-player game" to our "single-player game," where success and meaning are defined on our own terms. Growth may be uncomfortable at times, but embracing the rhythm of change allows us to navigate through awakening, expansion, stability, and closure with grace.

Contentment is the fruit-bearing result of all this growth. Contentment is the result of being aligned with your true self. Just as the fruit of a tree appears when the conditions are right, contentment blooms when what's inside matches what's outside. Contentment is the steady companion that remains when happiness comes and goes. It's neutrality and balance, finding peace between extremes. It's the Middle Path, the ability to observe life without judgment, to stay open and curious, no matter how twisted or backward life's events may seem. Ask The Farmer, and you'll understand: contentment is the fruit of a life well-lived.

Of course, we all face moments of self-sabotage. That's where resilience comes in. Tools like the Sage mindset or a personal "BS Meter" can help you cut through the noise and refocus on what matters. Gratitude and reframing are your allies in this process, reminding you to see challenges as opportunities for growth.

So, I invite you to imagine the wake of a drama-free life.

- What does the ripple look like to live in balance, guided by purpose, and aligned with my values?
- How does it feel to leave behind ripples of clarity and peace, not just for myself, but for all those around me?

I don't want you to think of this as just a book. It's a movement. One that goes straight to the root cause, cuts away the drama, and clears the path for truth and integrity. Contentment isn't the absence of challenge. It's the presence of clarity, intention, and grounded action.

We've got the tools. The path is right here, right now. The next chapter is ours to write. When we choose to live beyond the drama, we create a life of clarity, growth, and purpose.

Step forward, bold, grounded, and bulletproof into your next chapter.

"What is it you plan to do with your one wild and precious life?"

Life is continually ours to design. I am here with you.

Eric Stephenson

ABOUT
ERIC STEPHENSON

Eric Stephenson is on a mission to create kind, drama-free cultures where people thrive—in business and in life. His work takes him around the globe, helping replace conflict with connection and stress with sustainable performance.

With over 20 years as an entrepreneur, consultant, international speaker, and former Chief Wellness Officer for a 250-unit franchise system, Eric has led more than 500 live events as a keynote speaker, emotional intelligence strategist, and workshop facilitator. He has collaborated with world-class brands including Montage Resorts, Marriott International, Aescape, The Ritz-Carlton, Four Seasons, and Life Time Fitness.

Eric is the creator of The Kindness KPIs™—a measurable framework that transforms empathy, accountability, and resilience into strategic drivers of employee engagement, retention, and growth. In his free time, he pursues his dream of becoming the newest member of the Foo Fighters.

Contact Eric at eric@ericstephensonspeaks.com

Made in the USA
Columbia, SC
20 December 2025

76547292R00102